Seven Things That Steal Your Joy

Seven Things That Steal Your Joy

Overcoming the Obstacles to Your Happiness

JOYCE MEYER

WARNER
Faith

New York   Boston   Nashville

Warner Faith

Time Warner Book Group
1271 Avenue of the Americas, New York, NY 10020
Visit our Web site at www.twbookmark.com

The Warner Faith name and logo are registered trademarks of
Warner Books.

Printed in the United States of America

First International Trade Printing: April 2004
ISBN: 0-446-69342-1
10   9   8   7   6   5   4

Contents

〜

Contents

Note from the Author

───୨

I have a passion to help people enjoy their lives. I am sure it is partially due to the fact that I wasted a lot of years not enjoying mine. I actually grew up in an atmosphere in which I was made to feel guilty if I was enjoying myself. I became a workaholic and had a false sense of responsibility. God's Word has set me free and I want to help others find the truths that I have found.

Jesus certainly did not die for us so we could be joyless and miserable. He actually said in John 10:10 that He came so we could have life and enjoy it. Imagine that! Jesus wants us to *enjoy* life!

There are many things that can steal our joy. In this book we will cover seven of them. We will look at the "Joy Stealer" and the "Joy Keeper" of each area.

For instance, works of the flesh—in other words, our energy attempting to do God's job—is a major problem for many people, especially people who are rooted in "performance acceptance" principles. Like many other people I only felt acceptance from others, especially my father, when

I was performing well. Mistakes and flaws were not tolerated, nor was mercy given. Every benefit or kindness had to be earned.

I fell into the trap of "working" my way through life and "earning" everything. When I became a believer in Jesus Christ and entered into a relationship with Father God, I learned through studying the Bible that God wanted to take care of me. It was hard for me to let go and let God be God in my life. I did not know how to lean on Him so I continually struggled and felt frustrated.

God won't allow anything in our life to succeed unless we trust Him. Jesus said in John 15:5 that we can do nothing apart from Him.

Grace is God's ability, His energy and enablement, coming to us free of charge to help us do with ease what we could never do on our own. Works of the flesh must be given up in order for us to receive grace. Where works of the flesh exist, there is no joy. Frustration, struggle, and confusion are not God's will. You will find help for all these miseries in the pages of this book.

Jealousy, discontentment, reasoning, and many other things steal our joy, but thank God He teaches us to keep our joy. Satan is a thief, but Jesus died to bring the full restoration of everything man has lost through the deception of the enemy.

I spent a lot of time in years gone by learning to enjoy my life. The key word is *my* life. I learned not to covet someone else's life, but to enjoy mine. It has not been easy for me to make the transition. Nor am I saying that I am not still learning. But one thing I do know is that it is God's will for all of us to *enjoy* the life He has provided. The joy of the

Lord is our strength. We must make a decision to enjoy *everyday life*.

Enjoying life does not mean we have something exciting going on all the time; it simply means we need to learn to enjoy simple, everyday things. Most of life is rather ordinary, but we are supernaturally equipped with the power of God to live ordinary everyday life in an extraordinary way.

God is Life, and if we don't enjoy life, then we really don't enjoy Him. He came that we might have and enjoy our life to the full. Let's learn and take action so we can be a witness to the power of God that is available to all. Yes, it takes God's power to enjoy life because all of life is not easy. Many things happen that we did not plan and some of them are difficult. We all encounter people that are hard to deal with and situations that we deplore, yet Jesus said, "Cheer up, I have overcome the world and deprived it of the power to harm you" (See John 16:33). Cheer and joy are weapons of warfare, and sadness weakens us, but as I said earlier, joy strengthens.

I pray this book will be life changing for you and that as you become inspired by and with the joy of the Lord, you will in turn inspire others. Let's spread the good news that serving Jesus is a joyful thing! *Smile* and *laugh* . . . it makes you and everyone around you feel better.

—Joyce Meyer

INTRODUCTION

You Can Have Joy Every Day!

~~

Joy in life is a wonderful thing to have. Notice I said *in* life, not *with* life. We may want to see changes in our circumstances, but we don't have to allow unpleasant situations to make us miserable. Joy makes some of those less desirable circumstances more bearable.

For many years I did not enjoy my life, even as a Christian, but I wanted to—so I asked God to help me change. In this book I share the biblical truths through which I learned how to have joy every day. My purpose is to open the eyes of your understanding concerning the power of joy, how to get joy, and how to keep it.

Joy can vary in intensity from calm delight to extreme hilarity. It is closely connected to our expectations (what we think and believe). One meaning of *joy* is: "The passion or emotion excited by the acquisition or expectation of good."[1] In other words, our joy is affected by how much we *expect* good things to happen to us.

Joy is also closely connected to strength. Many people have no strength because they are seeking the happiness of the world instead of the joy of the Lord.

God's Word says, "Be not grieved and depressed, for the joy of the Lord is your strength and stronghold" (Nehemiah 8:10). The joy the Lord gives is not dependent on natural circumstances. God's Word teaches us about the joy of salvation (being happy because we are Christians)[2] and about having joy because of His Word and His presence.

The psalmist David wrote, "You will show me the path of life; in Your presence is fullness of joy, at Your right hand there are pleasures forevermore" (Psalm 16:11). The prophet Jeremiah said, "Your words are what sustain me. They bring me great joy and are my heart's delight" (Jeremiah 15:16 NLT). The apostle Paul tells us, "Rejoice in the Lord always [delight, gladden yourselves in Him]; again I say, Rejoice!"(Philippians 4:4).

All through the Bible, from cover to cover, we are encouraged to be joyful. We are told in Proverbs 17:22, "A merry heart doeth good like a medicine" (KJV). I think if people had more joy, they would probably be sick much less often. I believe joy does much more than just make us feel good; it strengthens our witness and improves our countenance, our health, and the quality of our lives.

But this is not a book about just happiness, joy, and health; it is also about *strength*. The joy of the Lord is our strength; it is our power to win—and our enemy, Satan, knows that.

Satan is an expert at stealing from us, but his favorite target is not our material possessions; it is our joy. He is always out to steal our joy because he knows if we lose our joy, we lose our strength, and that gives him a powerful advantage over us. So our joy is his main concern. He wants to bring discouraging things to our lives and make us believe that all life consists of is disappointments.

I used to feel disheartened about my life. When I was younger, I was a rather somber person. Having experienced a lot of hurt and emotional wounding, life was painful, joyless, and very serious to me. I always seemed to be carrying a heavy burden. I had to *learn* that I could enjoy life and be a happy, carefree, joyful individual.

It took me years to learn what I am going to share with you in this book. I hope that revealing these truths to you will help you to increase your joy and avoid the years of turmoil many of us go through before we learn how to get joy and keep it.

Remember, if you want to have any strength against Satan, you must keep your joy.

ENJOY LIFE

We don't have to let the devil take our joy away from us. No matter what is going on in our lives, we need to stay as happy as we can because then we will have the strength to face whatever comes our way.

One way we can stay happy is by not making a big deal out of little things that we should just let go. For example, maybe somebody did hurt our feelings, but getting angry will steal our joy; the answer is to get over it quickly.

"But what they did wasn't right," you may say.

We have all done something to somebody that wasn't right at some time in our life. When we did that, what did we need? We needed a little mercy. What did we want the person we offended to do for us? We wanted them to give us a break. That means we need to sow what we want to reap.[3]

Not only do we need to give other people a break, but we need to give ourselves a break. We need to learn not to be so hard on others or ourselves. Why? Because harshness and unforgiveness rob us of joy.

I believe it is extremely important that you enjoy your life. So in this book I want to share with you seven joy stealers and what you can do to stop Satan, the "joy thief," from stealing your joy. I also want to share with you how you can make some changes in the way you handle situations (if you need help in that area); otherwise, every time you turn around, you are going to be giving your joy to the enemy.

Do you want to be happier? Do you want to enjoy life to the fullest every day? I do. I want to enjoy every day I live. I don't want to enjoy life just every once in a while or just when things are going well. Even when I am having a big problem, I still want to enjoy life. I want to enjoy life while God is changing me. I want to enjoy life while He is bringing about my breakthrough. I want to enjoy life while my ministry is growing.

Like you, I want to enjoy life to the fullest—all of life, every day of life. And I have discovered that I am not going to do that if I am not *determined* to do it.

JOY IS A DECISION

The psalmist David said, "This is the day the LORD has made; we will rejoice and be glad in it" (Psalm 118:24 NKJV). I believe he was making a declaration, and he was establishing it not only for himself but for every one who wanted to listen.

Having joy is not about a feeling; it is about a decision. We can declare: "God has given me this day. And if He has decided to let me breathe another day, *then I am going to enjoy it.*"

Jesus said, "The thief comes only in order to steal and kill and destroy. I came that they may have and enjoy life, and have it in abundance (to the full, till it overflows)" (John 10:10).

Enjoying the abundant life Jesus died to give you is based on a decision you make, not on your circumstances. Decide to be happy right where you are and to enjoy the life you have right now on the way to where you're going.[4] Make a firm decision to enjoy your journey.

You can begin by saying out loud, "I am going to enjoy my life." Now say it like you really mean it: *"I am going to enjoy my life!"*

Until you get that thought established in your mind, every morning when you wake up, before you even get out of bed, I encourage you to declare out loud, "I am going to enjoy this day! I am seizing the day! I am taking authority over the devil, the joy thief, even before he tries to come against me! I have made up my mind that I am going to *keep my joy* today!"

It is my desire that you enjoy your life to overflowing, and I want to help you as much as I am able. In the first chapter of this book, we will compare the fruit of *working* to get what we want against simply *trusting* God's grace to give us His best.

Then I will show you seven Joy Stealers that rob us of the happiness God intends for us to enjoy. And for each Joy Stealer (works of the flesh, legalism, complicating simple events, excessive reasoning, anger, jealousy, and discontent), I will also show you a practical Joy Keeper to keep the devil from stealing your peace.

Before I learned the joy-keeping principles from God's Word that I am about to share with you, the devil was successful in stealing my joy and the enjoyment of life. I pray that the liberating truths in this book will not only prevent him from doing that in your life, but take you into a new realm of joy that will make him the loser instead of you.

Seven Things That Steal Your Joy

ONE

Two Choices: Works or Grace?

⁓

You have only one life to live, and you have a right to enjoy it. But one of the main things that will keep you from enjoying your life is works of the flesh. Works of the flesh are attempts to accomplish through your own energy things that are God's job.

And trying to do what only God can do always leads to frustration. Trusting God to do what only He can do always leads to joy because "what is impossible with men is possible with God" (Luke 18:27).

Jesus said, "My grace (My favor and loving-kindness and mercy) is enough for you [sufficient against any danger and enables you to bear the trouble manfully]; for My strength and power are made perfect (fulfilled and completed) and show themselves most effective in [your] weakness" (2 Corinthians 12:9).

We become frustrated when we try to achieve by *works* a life that God not only brought into being but designed to be received by *grace*. Grace is the power of God to meet our needs and solve our problems.[1]

1

I was living a frustrated, complicated, joyless life many years ago before I began to seriously seek God for answers to my problem of a lack of peace and joy. When I had a problem or a need, I tried to help myself and work things out in my own way, which never produced any good results. The Word of God and my personal experience have taught me that the way to avoid the frustration of fleshly works is to ask God for help.

LET GOD HELP YOU

At times, all of us are guilty of trying to handle our circumstances instead of trusting God to take care of them for us. It is not a sign of weakness to admit that we cannot help ourselves—it is the truth. Jesus said, "Apart from Me [cut off from vital union with Me] you can do nothing" (John 15:5).

You may be frustrated, struggling, and unhappy simply because you are trying to fix something you cannot do anything about. You may be trying to change something that only God can change. Perhaps you have a situation in your life that you don't want, and you are trying to get rid of it. If you are like most people, you will worry, fret, and work yourself to a frazzle until you realize that only God can get rid of it for you.

Maybe there is something you do want and are trying hard to get, yet nothing you try is working, and it is frustrating you. In that case, the only thing you can do is back off and wait on God. While you are waiting for God to take care of the situation, I encourage you to enjoy the wait. That may be hard because it takes patience, but it pays marvelous dividends in the end. Waiting on God honors Him, and the Bible says that the person who honors God will be honored by Him.[2]

LEAVE IT IN GOD'S HANDS

Suppose you feel you can't wait to get married, so you decide to find the perfect mate for yourself instead of waiting on God to work it out for you.

It would be a terrible mistake to become so desperate that you settle for someone who is not right for you. It would be much better to wait until God brings you a divine connection.

Maybe you are married, and you have been thinking, *I want my spouse to change. I just can't put up with my partner anymore.*

You cannot change your spouse; only God can. But God does not move in your life when you struggle and try to take matters into your own hands. He moves when you trust Him. So I suggest that you pray, cast your care on the Lord, leave your hands off the situation, trust God, and go ahead and enjoy your life.

It may not be a marital situation you want changed. You may feel that you want your kids to change, or you want more money, or you may want a different job.

We all have something going on in our lives we would like to see change for the better. Desiring change is just part of living.

You are always going to want something in your life to be different. So if you want an enjoyable life, sooner or later you must learn to quit trying to make things happen yourself.

Numerous times I struggled while trying to change my husband, trying to change my kids, trying to change myself, yet I failed every time. I probably struggled with changing myself more than anything or anyone else.

The truth is you can't really change yourself. You can only tell God that you want to change and that you are willing to change. You can only throw open your life to Him every day by praying, and leave the rest to Him.

Ask for God's help by praying this prayer:

Lord, work in me and change me. I know I can't do it myself. I know I can't make it happen, and it's not my place to make it happen. But I want You to do it, Lord, because I believe that only You can do it right.

In Mark 9:23, Jesus says that all things are possible to him who *believes*—not to him who comes up with a bright idea and a big plan and tries to make it work.

WORKS THAT DON'T WORK

The Word teaches that God's people dug wells for themselves that couldn't hold water: "My people have committed two evils: they have forsaken Me, the Fountain of living waters, and they have hewn for themselves cisterns, broken cisterns which cannot hold water" (Jeremiah 2:13). I know what it is like to work hard with no results. I have spent many years of my life digging empty wells like these, and I can tell you, it really wears you out.

You may be digging an empty well right now. You may be working on something or somebody. You may have your own little project going. You may be following your own little plan, trying to make things happen in your own strength and ability. If so, it is not going to work if you have left God out of your plan.

Many times we make a plan and then pray for it to work. God wants us to pray first and ask Him for His plan. After we have His plan, then He wants us to trust Him to bring it to pass.

Our activity birthed out of the flesh actually prevents God from showing Himself strong in our lives. The Bible describes that kind of activity as "works of the flesh."[3] I call them "works that don't work." That is not the way to live the higher life that God has prepared for us.

Two Ways to Live

We can live as a slave to the law, or as an heir to the promise of grace. The following passage presents two ways in which you and I can choose to live:

> For it is written that Abraham had two sons, one by the bondmaid and one by the free woman. But whereas the child of the slave woman was born according to the flesh and had an ordinary birth, the son of the free woman was born in fulfillment of the promise. Now all this is an allegory; these [two women] represent two covenants. One covenant originated from Mount Sinai [where the Law was given] and bears [children destined] for slavery; this is Hagar. (Galatians 4:22–24)

5

We know from studying Genesis chapters 11 through 21 that Sarah represents the other covenant mentioned in these verses.[4] She is the woman who was supposed to wait on the promise of God and receive the child born in a supernatural way.

Later in this book we will review how at one point Sarah grew tired of waiting for God's promise, tried to make things happen herself, and ended up in a mess. But God was faithful to keep His promise, and she found out that *when we wait on God and trust Him,* He will bring to pass what we are believing for according to His will—no matter how long it takes.

We can live by trying to take care of ourselves, or we can live by trusting God. We can try to make things happen, or we can believe God to make things happen. The choice is ours.

If you want the pressure taken off, then choose to stop trying to make everything happen yourself, in your own timing, in your own way, according to your own plan. Instead, throw your life wide open to God and pray:

Lord, whatever I may desire in life, if You don't want me to have it, I don't want it. If You do want me to have it, I ask You for it and believe You will give it to me in Your time, in Your way, according to Your divine plan.

In my own life, I have adopted a new policy. It's called the hands-off policy. Every day I pray: *Lord, I am not doing anything unless You show me what You want me to do.*

I believe if you ask God for this kind of guidance, you will see marvelous things happen in your life.

DON'T WORK TO CHANGE OTHERS

As I said before, I tried so long to change my husband, but it never really helped. As a matter of fact, it only made things worse because people rebel when they know someone is trying to remodel them.

People want to have the freedom to be who they are. Everyone wants a little space. No one wants to have to endure judgment and criticism from somebody else who is constantly trying to rework them.

Finally, Dave and I made an agreement that we would stop trying to change each other because, otherwise, our marriage wasn't going to work.

The fact is that God made men and women to be different, and He did that on purpose. We are to help build each other up where we have frailties, but we are not called to change our differences. We are in each other's lives to encourage each other to become all God has in mind for us to be.

If God has given you a marriage partner who seems very different from you, most likely He did that because your spouse has some gift or ability or characteristic that you don't have but *need*. Together you complement each other with your strengths and depend on each other in your areas of weakness.[5]

"But my partner drives me crazy," you may say.

Well, you probably drive your partner crazy, too.

Many couples are divorcing today because they say they are not compatible. But the truth is that in the natural, there are no two people in the world who are 100 percent compatible.

7

The Word says, "Therefore a man shall leave his father and his mother and shall become united and cleave to his wife, and they shall become one flesh" (Genesis 2:24). It sounds so easy when you read in the Bible that a man will leave his mother and father and cleave to his wife, and the two of them will become one flesh. The leaving and cleaving part is not usually difficult. It is the part about *becoming one* that is the problem.

I can now say that Dave and I have become one flesh. But in the beginning it was not any fun. I was trying to change him, he was trying to change me, and we had all kinds of problems.

Dave was laid back and didn't worry about anything; to him everything was okay. I was always worrying about everything. For example, I would be in the kitchen counting up the money and the bills—and there would always be more bills than money. While I was in there worrying, Dave would be in the living room playing with the kids. That made me mad because I wanted him to come into the kitchen and worry with me.

I would ask him, "Why should you be in there enjoying yourself while I've got all this burden on me?"

"You don't have to have the burden; nobody told you to do that," he would say. "We tithe. We give. We're doing what God is telling us to do. God takes care of us. Don't worry. Come in here and play with us."

Oh, no, I had to worry. I had to try to figure out where the money was going to come from to pay all those bills. I would say, "Well, if God is going to give it to us, who is He going to give it to us through, and how is He going to give it to us, and when is it going to come?" Perhaps you recognize these symptoms of worry in yourself:

"Why, God, why?"

"When, God, when?"

"How, God, how?"

"Who, God, who?"

I wanted answers. I didn't want to trust; I wanted to know. I wanted a blueprint laid out in front of me for everything because I didn't really know how to trust God.

ARE YOU RESTLESS OR RESTING?

The Bible teaches us that those who believe God enter into His rest. That is one way you can tell whether you are really *in* faith, or whether you are just trying to *have* faith. When you enter into the realm of faith, you enter into the rest of God: "We who have believed (adhered to and trusted in and relied on God) do enter that rest" (Hebrews 4:3).

Rest is freedom from excessive reasoning, struggle, fear, inner turmoil, worry, and frustration, which develop because of our working to do what only God can do. Being in God's rest is not resting from physical activity but resting in confidence in the midst of everything that goes on in life. It is a rest of the soul—the mind, will, and emotions being at peace.

You can rest in God because you know He is going to take care of you and meet your need. You don't know when or how, and you really don't care because you are enjoying the life you have right now while God is working on your problem.

God wants us to live that way. But to do that, we have to "believe that God exists and that He is the rewarder of those who earnestly and diligently seek Him [out]" (Hebrews 11:6).

Dave and I are about as different as any two people can be, and yet we have learned to get along with one another. We have learned to respect each other's differences. We work on so many projects together that we have to trust God.

What about you? Which way do you want to live? Do you want to live by God's promise, or do you want to live by struggle?

I believe God has you reading this book so you will make a decision about how you want to live your life. If you are worn out, I urge you to enter into God's rest. I encourage you to quit trying to control everyone and everything around you and simply allow God to do for you what only He can do.

No matter what you face, God wants to help you.

After His Son, Jesus, died on the cross for our sins, was resurrected from the grave, and ascended into heaven, God sent the Holy Spirit to be in close fellowship with us. If you have invited Jesus into your heart,* the Holy Spirit is your Helper, and He is standing by to give you comfort and aid.[6] That means you don't ever have to face your problems alone.

I have learned that even if I get into trouble through a

---

*If you have never invited Jesus to live in your heart but would like to confess Him as your Savior, there is a prayer you can pray at the back of this book.

lack of wisdom or some fleshly disobedience, I don't have to face it by myself. I can turn back to God for help, and He won't let me down.

In the next chapter, we will look at two people in the Bible who found out for themselves that a work of the flesh is a Joy Stealer.

TWO

Joy Stealer #1: Works of the Flesh

⁓

The following verses begin to relate the story of Abraham and Sarah, whose works of the flesh complicated their promise of joy:

The word of the Lord came to Abram in a vision, saying, Fear not, Abram, I am your Shield, your abundant compensation, and your reward shall be exceedingly great.

And Abram said, Lord God, what can You give me, since I am going on [from this world] childless and he who shall be the owner and heir of my house is this [steward] Eliezer of Damascus? . . . Look, You have given me no child; and [a servant] born in my house is my heir.

And behold, the word of the Lord came to him, saying, This man shall not be your heir, but he who shall come from your own body shall be your heir. . . . Look now toward the heavens and count the stars—if you are able to number them. Then He said to him, So shall your descendants be.

And he [Abram] believed in (trusted in, relied on,

remained steadfast to) the Lord, and He counted it to him as righteousness (right standing with God). (Genesis 15:1–6)

This is such an awesome story. God tells Abraham, "I am going to bless you," and Abraham replies, "Lord, what can You give me that I could possibly want? If I don't have a child, I will have nobody to leave it to anyway."

We hear the cry of Abraham's heart in this passage. He is saying, "Lord, I don't care what else You give me; what I really want is a child. Please give me an heir."

What Abraham really wanted was a son. For you it may be something else. You may be saying, "Lord, I don't care what You give me because nothing else is going to make me happy if You don't change my marriage. Please give me a happy marriage."

I went through a long period of time where no matter what God did for me, it really didn't mean anything to me if my ministry was not going to grow, if I wasn't going to see my dream fulfilled.

I got into major works of the flesh trying to make my ministry become what it is today. But no matter what I did, no matter how hard I worked, it still stayed pitifully little. I didn't like little; I wanted big. I read in the Bible that I was not to despise these small beginnings,[1] but I despised them anyway. At times I would get so frustrated I would think, *Oh, God, either do something to make my ministry grow—or let it die!*

Do you feel called into ministry? If so, are you going through some of what I experienced? Do you feel that God has put you up on a shelf somewhere and forgotten about you? Do you have some other big dream and vision, and yet nothing or little is happening?

God wanted to use me in ministry, but before He could do that, He had to change me. I had a ministry gift to teach, but I didn't have strong character or lasting fruit of the Spirit.

Fruit of the Spirit is described in the Bible as love, joy, peace, patience, kindness, goodness, faithfulness, gentleness (humility), and self-control.[2] Gifts for ministry are *given*,[3] but fruit is *developed*. To produce fruit, we must go through trials to test our faith.

Paul encouraged believers to rejoice in the midst of trials, saying:

> Moreover [let us also be full of joy now!] let us exult and triumph in our troubles and rejoice in our sufferings, knowing that pressure and affliction and hardship produce patient and unswerving endurance. And endurance (fortitude) develops *maturity of character* (approved faith and tried integrity). And *character [of this sort] produces [the habit of] joyful and confident hope* of eternal salvation. (Romans 5:3–4, italics mine)

God had put the gift in me; I could preach and teach many years ago just as I can now. But God didn't allow me to minister all over the world then the way He has today because I would have done a lot of damage. I didn't have maturity of character, and I didn't have the fruit of His Spirit.

When you are on television worldwide as I am, everywhere you go people recognize you. So I have learned that I had better be walking the walk and not just talking the talk or I am going to hurt a lot of people. I can't just tell other people what the Word of God says to do—I need to be doing it, too. I need to be an example. God had to do a major work *in* me before He could do any work *through* me. He had to develop in me the fruit of the Spirit, which is mature character.

I don't have enough time or space to tell you all the things I went through trying to get from where I started out as a messed-up, abused, angry, bitter, resentful young girl to where I am today. I can tell you that along the way I probably cried a swimming pool full of tears, but it was worth it. I am a good person to listen to not just because I have preached a sermon or written a book, but because I have lived through what I talk about.

In this book I am sharing with you a piece of my life. I have learned through personal experience that *works of the flesh don't work*. I couldn't make my ministry grow. And God did not let it grow until I said sincerely, "Lord, I would like for my ministry to grow, but if it never does grow, I am happy with You."

When we want something so badly that we cannot be happy without it, it is no longer a normal, godly desire. It has become a lust. If there is anything in life that is more important to us than God, He is not going to give it to us.

"What If I Never Get It?"

As we see in the following Scriptures, God was testing Abraham's faith when He told Abraham to sacrifice his beloved son Isaac (the heir God had given him after so many years of waiting):

After these events, God tested and proved Abraham and said to him, Abraham! And he said, Here I am.

[God] said, Take now your son, your only son Isaac, whom you love, and go to the region of Moriah; and offer him there as a burnt offering upon one of the mountains of which I will tell you.

So Abraham rose early in the morning, saddled his donkey, and took two of his young men with him and his son Isaac; and he split the wood for the burnt offering, and then began the trip to the place of which God had told him. (Genesis 22:1–3)

I believe God was also testing Abraham's priorities. Isaac had probably become very important to Abraham, so God tested Abraham to see if he would give up Isaac to Him in faith and obedience.[4] When God saw Abraham's willingness to obey, He provided a ram for Abraham to sacrifice in place of Isaac.[5]

Remember, we all go through tests. As with Abraham, these tests are designed to try, prove, and develop our faith.[6] One of the tests I had to face was: "What if I never have the ministry I've dreamed about for so long? What if I never get to minister to more than fifty people at a time? Can I still love God and be happy?"

What about you? If you never get the thing you are believing for, can you still love God and be happy?

You have to get to the point where you can be happy without having what you want, or you will never receive it.

You may want to get married. What if you never get married? Can you be happy anyway?

You may want a certain person in your family to change.

What if that individual never changes? Can you be happy anyway?

You may want to make more money. What if you never have any more money than what you have right now? Can you be happy anyway?

If you don't get whatever it is you want, can you still love God? Will you still serve Him all the days of your life? Or are you just trying to get something from Him? A fine line divides the motives of the heart between selfish and selfless; and we must always make sure we understand which side of the line we are standing on.

God wants you to have abundant blessings, but there is something you have to do to receive them: Keep God first in your life! God "will give them to you if you give him first place in your life and live as he wants you to" (Matthew 6:33 TLB). If you keep God first in your life, He doesn't really mind how much else you have because He loves you and wants to radically bless you. He delights in the prosperity of His children.[7]

There are pitifully few people God can bless radically. Those people are the ones who keep Him first in their lives. That is difficult for some of us to do because once the blessings start rolling in, all of a sudden those things can become more important to us than God. That's why we have to be very careful in this area.

"Why Does God Wait So Long?"

I really enjoy what God is allowing me to do in ministry, but I try not to let my self-worth become tied up in it. The reason is that if someday I am not able to do this anymore, I still want to have joy. I still want to enjoy my life. I still want to know that I am a valuable person.

When God came to Abraham and told him that He was going to bless him, Abraham said to God, "That's fine, but what I really want is a son."

God said, "I am going to give you what you ask for," but He didn't give it to Abraham right away. The Word says, "Abraham was a hundred years old when Isaac was born" (Genesis 21:5). Actually, twenty years went by from the time God promised Abraham that he would have a child to the time that child was born. In fact, Abraham was already old when God first gave him the promise of a son.

By the time Abraham fathered that child, his wife had already gone through the change of life. She had a barren womb. So Abraham and Sarah not only had a prayer request, they also needed a miracle.

Isn't it interesting that sometimes when you ask God for something, He lets it go so long, the only thing that can possibly produce what you asked for is a miracle? Why does God do that? Because He likes "to show Himself strong in behalf of those whose hearts are blameless toward Him" (2 Chronicles 16:9).

When Martha and Mary sent for Jesus to come and minister to their brother, Lazarus, who was gravely ill, why did Jesus wait two days longer, until Lazarus had actually died and was buried, before He went and raised Lazarus from the dead?[8] It was because Jesus already knew what He was going to do for Lazarus.

If something is dead—a dream, a desire, a want, a need—it doesn't matter to God how dead it is. God can still bring it back to life in His timing because our God is an awesome God. Nothing is too hard for Him.[9] That is why He is never in a hurry and why it seems as if He often waits until nothing will work but a miracle.

"WHAT CAN I DO TO SPEED THINGS UP?"

Sarah and Abraham became tired of waiting for their promised child. Then Sarah had this bright idea:

> Now Sarai, Abram's wife, had borne him no children. She had an Egyptian maid whose name was Hagar. And Sarai said to Abram, See here, the Lord has restrained me from bearing [children]. I am asking you to have intercourse with my maid; it may be that I can obtain children by her. And Abram listened to and heeded what Sarai said. (Genesis 16:1–2)

Do you see what happened here? Sarah thought she could work out a plan to achieve God's promise. Most of us are like that when we have been waiting for something for a long time. We say, "Oh, I know what I can do," and we try to speed things up, as Sarah did. But all we end up doing is stretching out our waiting time.

I understand that Sarah desperately wanted a child, but when it began to look as if it was not going to happen, these next verses show that she did something that was just plain foolish:

> So Sarai, Abram's wife, took Hagar her Egyptian maid, after Abram had dwelt ten years in the land of Canaan, and gave her to her husband Abram to be his [second-ary] wife. And he had intercourse with Hagar, and she became pregnant; and when she saw that she was with child, she looked with contempt upon her mistress and despised her.
>
> Then Sarai said to Abram, May [the responsibility for] my wrong and deprivation of rights be upon you! I gave my maid into your bosom, and when she saw that she was with child, I was contemptible and despised in her eyes. May the Lord be the judge between you and me. (Genesis 16:3–5)

Now, any woman who would give her maid to her husband to be his secondary wife is so desperate that she is just not thinking clearly.

Notice that Hagar developed an attitude. Before she became pregnant by Abraham, she was a submissive handmaid. But as soon as she saw that she was going to have Abraham's child, she thought she had the upper hand over Sarah. So she began to treat Sarah with contempt and disrespect.

Oh, yes, these were people just like us.

That was when the trouble started. When Sarah saw Hagar's changed attitude toward her because of what had happened, Sarah blamed it all on Abraham. She had started the whole mess and talked Abraham into it, but suddenly it was his fault because Sarah was having trouble with her maid.

In Genesis 16:6 we read, "But Abram said to Sarai, See here, your maid is in your hands and power; do as you please with her."

Abraham was in essence saying, "I have nothing to do with all this. It isn't my problem; it's yours. You handle it."

Isn't that similar to what happened in the Garden of Eden when Adam and Eve disobeyed God and ate of the forbidden fruit?[10] Didn't Adam blame Eve for tempting him into eating some of that fruit, and didn't Eve blame the serpent for tempting her into eating it? Everybody was passing the buck to somebody else, and nobody wanted to take any responsibility.

Isn't that what we do when we make a mess in our lives? When we get into works of the flesh, we find ourselves in a big mess that has to be dealt with. Then we find someone else to blame. Usually, like Eve, we say, "It's all the devil's fault."

Before I learned to take responsibility for the consequences of my own actions, I blamed the devil for everything that went wrong in my life. I rebuked him until my "rebuker" was worn out. But the devil still didn't leave me alone.

I was constantly saying, "I rebuke you, Satan. I rebuke you. Get out, devil! I rebuke you."

But no matter how much I blamed Satan and rebuked the devil, I kept having the same problems. If that describes your situation, the cause of your problem may be an "Ishmael."

ARE YOU TAKING CARE OF AN ISHMAEL?

God promised to multiply Abraham and make him the father of many nations even after the birth of Hagar's baby, who was named Ishmael:

> When Abram was ninety-nine years old, the Lord appeared to him and said, I am the Almighty God; walk and live habitually before Me and be perfect (blameless, wholehearted, complete). And I will make My covenant (solemn pledge) between Me and you and will multiply you exceedingly.
>
> Then Abram fell on his face, and God said to him, As for Me, behold, My covenant (solemn pledge) is with you, and you shall be the father of many nations. Nor shall your name any longer be Abram [high, exalted father]; but your name shall be Abraham [father of a multitude], for I have made you the father of many nations. (Genesis 17:1–5)

It had been nearly twenty years since God first promised a son to Abraham and Sarah. All this time, Abraham and his family had been taking care of Ishmael, trying to raise him.

Ishmael was a man of war and was engaged in warfare most of his life. Hagar and Sarah had been fighting, and Abraham had been caught in the middle. I am sure it was not a fun time for any of them. Although it is not recorded in the Bible, it is easy to imagine what it must have been like around Abraham's house during that period. By this time, Abraham and Sarah were wondering about the child God had promised them. I am sure they could not understand

22

why it was taking God so long to fulfill His promise to them.

I don't think they would have had to wait twenty years if they had not had Ishmael. If they had not become impatient and made their own plan, which resulted in Ishmael's birth, I think the birth of Isaac would have taken place much sooner.

As did Abraham and Sarah, once we have given birth to an Ishmael, we have to spend many years taking care of it. Once we have complicated our lives, it takes a while to clean things up.

Have you ever made a mess that took you longer to get out of than it did to get into? Have you done some things in your life that you wish you hadn't done?

Most of us have, and consequences follow every action. If you are dealing with the consequences of an Ishmael, it does not mean that God will not bless you. But those consequences may delay receiving God's best for your life.

THE LAUGH OF FAITH OR DOUBT?

God made Sarah the *mother of nations* just as He had made Abraham *the father of many nations*:

> And God said to Abraham, As for Sarai your wife, you shall not call her name Sarai; but Sarah [Princess] her name shall be. And I will bless her and give you a son also by her. Yes, I will bless her, and she shall be a mother of nations; kings of peoples shall come from her.

23

Then Abraham fell on his face and laughed. (Genesis 17:15–17)

By this time Sarah had gone through the change of life and was old and perhaps wrinkled; she probably looked like anything but a princess. Yet God told Abraham, "From now on I want you to call your wife a princess." I believe this helped Sarah to see herself as God saw her and made it easier for her to release her faith and receive from God.

When God told Abraham that he would have a son by Sarah in their old age, Abraham laughed. But it was not a doubting laugh; it was the laugh of faith.[11]

Later on, in Genesis chapter 18, the Lord tells Abraham that in the next season Sarah will bear him a son. Sarah's faith had probably been affected by the long delay, and when she heard God speak that word to Abraham, she also laughed. But hers was not the laugh of faith; it was the laugh of doubt.[12] Sarah's faith needed to be encouraged and built up.

I believe when we learn to live under the covenant of promise, as Abraham did, we can also laugh the laugh of faith. The bottom line is if you want to have laughter and joy in your life, stop living by works of the flesh and start living by the promises of God. Stop trying to make things happen yourself. Tell God what you want, believe what He says about it in His Word, and let Him bring it to pass.

How can you tell when you are into works of the flesh?

As soon as you start struggling and trying to make something happen, and then you become frustrated because it is not happening, you are into works of the flesh. For example, you may say, "I asked for a promotion at work, and I didn't get it. I rebuked Satan and got angry at the person who was promoted because that person didn't deserve it, and I did."

That attitude may be the reason you weren't given the promotion. Many times, our attitudes toward our circumstances can keep us from having the blessings God wants to give us.

God is much more concerned about changing our attitudes than He is about giving us a promotion. Psalm 75:6–7 tells us that true promotion comes from God. Reaching the place where you can be happy for other people who are blessed will lead you into God's blessings for you.

THE LAUGH OF FAITH

Abraham knew he was old, and he knew Sarah's barren condition, and *yet he believed God anyway:*

> [For Abraham, human reason for] hope being gone, hoped in faith that he should become the father of many nations, as he had been promised, so [numberless] shall your descendants be. He did not weaken in faith when he considered the [utter] impotence of his own body, which was as good as dead because he was about a hundred years old, or [when he considered] the barrenness of Sarah's [deadened] womb. No unbelief or distrust made him waver (doubtingly question) concerning the promise of God, but he grew strong and was empowered by faith as he gave praise and glory to God. (Romans 4:18–20)

When Abraham heard the promise of God, he laughed. It made him joyful to realize that God could do something that was impossible:

> The Lord visited Sarah as He had said, and the Lord did for her as He had promised. For Sarah became pregnant and bore Abraham a son in his old age, at the set time God had told him. Abraham named his son whom Sarah bore to him Isaac [laughter]. (Genesis 21:1–3)

Isaac brought laughter to his parents because he was the fulfillment of a work of God.

I can relate to that. Without God's help, it is impossible for me to stand in front of people and minister the Word of God to them. It is a miracle because of where I came from and how big a mess I was when God spoke to my heart so many years ago about having this ministry. And it makes me laugh. I spent so many years frowning and being sad all the time because of works of the flesh. Now I have a big smile on my face most of the time.

Works that don't work will steal your joy. The promise of God will leave you laughing. Trying to speed things up to get what God has promised to give you is a work of the flesh, and this Joy Stealer will leave you frustrated and fruitless. The decision is yours. Which will you choose?

In the next chapter I will show you how you can combat a work of the flesh by being led of the Spirit.

THREE

Joy Keeper #1: Be Led of the Spirit

~

One of the most dynamic ways to keep our joy is to allow the Holy Spirit to lead us in the way we should go. If we pray first and ask God for a plan, He will never push us into a work of the flesh. Instead, His Holy Spirit prompts, guides, and gently leads us to a place of joy; He will never manipulate or control us. If we are too consumed with our own plan, too locked into the way we think things ought to be, we won't even hear God speak to us or recognize that those promptings we feel are from Him. If we are too determined to follow our own ritualistic rules, we can miss the gentle leading of the Holy Spirit and lose the joy that God intends for us to have (see 2 Cor. 3:17).

God has an individual plan for each one of our days. God cares about every day that we live, and His plan for us is good. I believe it is wise to have a plan and to work the plan. If people don't have any kind of plan, they never do anything.

It doesn't work to be vague and unfocused. It wouldn't be wise for me to step out in front of my audiences without a plan, or show up and say, "I'm just going to be led of the Spirit." I think about what I am going to say, because nobody wants to stand up to speak and have nothing to say!

It would be foolish for me to show up at my conferences without preparing a message or studying the Word. On the other hand, if I am visiting somewhere and am invited to share something unexpectedly, then I can still trust God's leading to use me and give me something relevant for the situation I am in. In both situations, with or without a plan, I have learned to ask, "Now God, what do *You* want me to say? What do You want me to do?"

SEEK GOD'S WAY

Joy comes when we seek God's way, not our own way. It is so important to learn to obey God and go the way He tells us to go. If God says turn to the right or turn to the left, we need to be trained well enough that we are willing to ditch our own plans as soon as we feel God's leading.

God will lead you if you have done your part to plan, but be willing to set your plan aside if He leads you another way. There is a fine balance in working on your plan, but then trusting God to lead you through His *perfect* plan. The minute you sense there is no grace (no power) working through your plan, you should look for God's leading.

The Lord revealed through the prophet Zechariah that He would work in the lives of His people, saying, "Not by might, nor by power, but by My Spirit [of Whom the oil is a symbol], says the Lord of hosts." God promised to "bring forth the finishing gable stone [of the new temple] with loud shoutings of the people, crying, Grace, grace to it!" (Zechariah 4:6–7).

Grace is the ability of the Holy Spirit to make something work that would otherwise be either difficult or even impossible for us to do without His help. If we try to do something without that grace, it will be hard, laborious, and very frustrating.

Many people who are called to do things don't know how to tap into the grace of God; therefore, they struggle their whole lives trying to do something that God would delight in making easy for them if they would only seek His grace.

We have to learn how to be sensitive to God's anointing. For example, we plan to sing certain songs in our conferences, but if we sense there is no anointing, my worship leader changes gears and leads us in songs that are relevant to what God is doing on that particular day. He does an excellent job of following God's leading. If he was not willing to lay aside his plan, he would not be able to usher people into the presence of God. To walk in the presence of God, we must give the Holy Spirit the right-of-way.

When I study the Word to plan a message, it amazes me how God helps me pick the right message for every session. As I study, I might prepare five messages for the seminars, but I won't know exactly which one I'm supposed to preach on Thursday night, which one Friday morning, or which one Friday night. I don't just line them up a certain way. I have learned to wait on God to lead me in His plan. I have learned to sense whether or not a message is right for the people who have come for ministry. What isn't right for one night may be a perfect plan for the next morning.

Sometimes when I study the message I plan for the opening session, I can tell it does not feel right, so I preach something else. But then I may feel led to share that message the next day. We have learned that it is not the thing we are doing that is so important, it is whether God has anointed it. And it is not that certain messages and songs aren't anointed; they may just not be part of God's plan for a particular time.

Our obedience to God's plan will usher people into His presence. We need to understand that when God anoints the things we do, we find joy through the Holy Ghost.

On one occasion during a service, I had just started reading Psalm 91 and unexpectedly preached the whole message from that chapter. That was several years ago, but people still ask for that tape because God chose to anoint that message at that time.

Too much structure to a plan can quench the move of God. For example, if we restrict the number of minutes we allow for each part of a conference, we can wind up with a dead and dry service. We need to know how to give way to the Holy Spirit.

God could give us a plan before the service and anoint that, but He doesn't always work that way. Sometimes I think God purposely hides His plan just to keep us "walking on water." When we are not so prepared, we are more dependent on Him. That way, we stay focused on Him instead of on our own plan.

Many of my experiences in ministry are examples of the way God leads us in the businesses or tasks He has called us to do. When God tells us to do something, He intends for us to step out, not to go get "a plan." And after we step out, God will give us His plan. But do you know how He gives it to us? One step at a time. We want the whole blueprint for the next twenty years laid out in front of us before we step out and do something. But God doesn't work like that, and we will never find joy if we think we have to know everything before we take our first step in the direction He is leading us.

I'm not saying God never lays the whole thing out in front of us, because sometimes He does. But everything we do with God and for God and through God has to be done by faith or it is of no value.

The Bible says we can't please God without faith. God wants to impact our lives, but we need to let go of our own ways to allow Him to do so. I don't mean for just one time; following God's leading needs to be our ongoing lifestyle.

"A man's mind plans his way, but the Lord directs his steps *and* makes them sure" (Proverbs 16:9). God might lead us to do something one way for twenty years, but then He may suddenly be finished with that method of working through us. Out of habit, we can carry around all kinds of dead bones because we don't want to let go of something God is finished with. We need to understand that God might want us to do something else.

BE WILLING TO MAKE CHANGES

God may lead you to do something with a certain group of people every Wednesday morning for five years. You may love it and believe it is wonderful, but then, all of a sudden, it seems dry and lifeless, and you wonder what is wrong with you. You continue to do the same thing, but you stop enjoying it. If you are not careful, you will start to be a faultfinder.

It is probably one of the hardest things in the world for people to walk away from doing something they have done for a long time. I don't mean just church programs, but when we grow used to doing things a certain way it can be difficult to let the Lord lead us to a new and better way.

In many ways, I can't stand to do the same thing for too long. For example, I have several pairs of pajamas because I just don't like to look at the same ones all the time. But in certain areas I'm not like that—I would probably be happy with the same hairstyle till Jesus comes!

If we do the same thing the same way too long, it just becomes old and stale, and it means nothing. But one of the things I have learned about the Holy Spirit is that if we follow Him, He keeps everything fresh. Life does not get stale when we follow the Lord. The Holy Spirit will lead us to change things on purpose just to make us pay attention to Him. God may lead you to simply take a different route home from work. He may want to show you a new tree or something beautiful on your way home.

Don't just keep doing things the same way if you are no longer joyful when you do them. You will lose your joy if you are not willing to get out of the boat. If you have already lost your joy, God may be dealing with you to make some changes.

You may be thinking, *But what if I sink?*

I believe God has led you to read this book to encourage you to take a step of faith and just do whatever it is that God has been telling you to do. He wants to restore your joy.

The Word says, "The plans of the mind and orderly thinking belong to man, but from the Lord comes the [wise] answer of the tongue" (Proverbs 16:1). Sometimes the biggest messes are made by all our planning for what we are going to do or say to people.

Don't become so locked into your plan that God can't speak to or through you. As an interesting Scripture states, "I know that [the determination of] the way of a man is not in himself; it is not in man [even in a strong man or in a man at his best] to direct his [own] steps" (Jeremiah 10:23). In other words, we are not smart enough to run our own lives.

REST YOUR MIND

Are you a big thinker? Does your mind race all the time with worry about whether or not you are doing everything right? The Word says, "Many plans are in a man's mind, but it is the Lord's purpose for him that will stand" (Proverbs 19:21).

Some people may not think enough, but God doesn't want us to fill our thoughts by planning works of the flesh that are not part of His plan. He wants us to seek His face and find His purpose for our lives.

My brain used to be like a busy freeway before I learned to stop trying to reason everything out ahead of time. I wanted to be in control by doing everything I knew to do right, but I learned that we don't really walk with God in faith unless we trust Him to lead us each step of the way.

The Word says, "Without faith it is impossible to please and be satisfactory to Him" (Hebrews 11:6). We have to trust God. Trusting God pleases Him. Trusting God requires unanswered questions. If we know everything, there is no need to trust God.

I know what I plan to do today, and I believe I know in general what I will be doing the rest of this year. But which one of us can really say we are absolutely, 100 percent confident that we know how our lives are going to go?

James emphasized the importance of being led of the Spirit when he wrote:

> Come now, you who say, Today or tomorrow we will go into such and such a city and spend a year there and carry on our business and make money. Yet you do not know [the least thing] about what may happen tomorrow. What is the nature of your life? You are [really] but a wisp of vapor (a puff of smoke, a mist) that is visible for a little while and then disappears [into thin air]. You ought instead to say, If the Lord is willing, we shall live and we shall do this or that [thing]. (James 4:13–15)

It's All About Balance

We need to be balanced when it comes to planning, but I believe some people need to be delivered from excessive planning. The Bible says, "Be well balanced (temperate, sober of mind), be vigilant and cautious at all times; for that enemy of yours, the devil, roams around like a lion roaring [in fierce hunger], seeking someone to seize upon and devour" (1 Peter 5:8). As I said before, it is good to have a plan, but if the plan becomes a work of the flesh, it will steal our joy.

One of the ways I can tell I'm planning excessively is if my plan starts to become a burden to me. If I start wearing myself out with thinking, then I realize I need to open my mind to learn something new God wants me to know. When He leads us, we stay refreshed all the time.

It's all about balance. Even in ministry, we don't have to be pressing and pushing all the time. God wants us to enjoy what we are doing. Jesus died so we could have abundant life—a good life complete with some enjoyment. He didn't die just so we could work hard all the time. I believe there is a way to do what God calls us to do, and yet have extreme, radical joy in doing it. God said, "For I know the thoughts and plans that I have for you, says the Lord, thoughts and plans for welfare and peace and not for evil, to give you hope in your final outcome" (Jeremiah 29:11).

The Word also speaks of God's plan for the world:

Making known to us the mystery (secret) of His will (of His plan, of His purpose). [And it is this:] In accordance with His good pleasure (His merciful intention) which He had previously purposed and set forth in Him, [He planned] for the maturity of the times and the climax of the ages to unify all things and head them up and consummate them in Christ, [both] things in heaven and things on the earth. (Ephesians 1:9–10)

God has a corporate plan for the body of Christ, but He also has a daily plan for each believer. Just as God has a plan for each of our lives, He also has a plan for each service that is called together in His name.

God doesn't want us to just sing songs when we come together; He wants us to praise and worship Him. During that time of praise and worship, He wants to minister to people's needs and break the yoke of bondage from them. God wants people to be set free from the grip of Satan and pulled out of the doors of hell.

It is useless to follow dead works instead of the living plan of God. He doesn't anoint tradition; He anoints those who are living in a close relationship with Him. If you're cooperating with the Holy Ghost, no one can keep God from doing through you what God wants to do. God will make His plan work. If you have a call on your life, you don't have to worry about whether or not you will get to do what God has called you to do.

Many years ago, when I didn't understand the kinds of things I am teaching now, I was strong-willed, bullheaded, and a quick decision maker. I had a call on my life, and I was sensing deep in my spirit what God wanted me to do. I could sense what God wanted, but I didn't have the foggiest idea how I was really supposed to get from here to there, so I started working on a plan.

But God said, "Joyce, you think you're so smart. You think you know everything. You've got your little plan and you think you know exactly what I'm going to do and how I'm going to do it. But let Me tell you something—you don't know half what you think you know."

God brought this Scripture to my memory: "In all your ways know, recognize, and acknowledge Him, and He will direct and make straight and plain your paths. Be not wise in your own eyes; reverently fear and worship the Lord and turn [entirely] away from evil" (Proverbs 3:6–7).

It is so easy to start making a plan instead of waiting on God to get *His* plan. Then we make our plan a rule without even acknowledging God. But the proverb says to acknowledge God in *all our ways*, so this would include *all our plans*.

Acknowledging God takes a little bit of time. *Acknowledge* means "to recognize the rights, authority, or status of; to disclose knowledge of or agreement with; to express gratitude or obligation for; to take notice of; to make known the receipt of; to recognize as genuine or valid."[1] To acknowledge God, we must slow down long enough to pray. We must ask Him, "God, what do You care about this? What do You think about this?" Then we must wait on Him for His answer.

If we wait on Him, the anointing will come to make His plan happen. He will direct us in the way we should go. If you keep your plan before the Lord, you must be ready to let Him change anything at anytime. If you do this, your path will always be right and prosperous.

ACKNOWLEDGE GOD

I have a certain place where I like to pray every morning. That's the first place I go, and it is of primary importance to me that I spend time with God. But even prayer can become a work of the flesh if I pray only out of habit rather than honestly desiring God's direction.

We will miss out on an intimate relationship with God if we make prayer a work of the flesh, saying, "Okay now, I'm going to pray for fifteen minutes, and I'm going to read the Word for twenty minutes, and I'm going to pray in the Spirit for five minutes,[2] and I'm going to confess the Word for ten minutes, and then I'll have done my duty."

We know we are being led of the Spirit when we *want* to pray, when we *want* to study the Word, and when we *want* to receive God's discipline. True joy is found when we can feel the touch of God on our plans. The Word says, "I will give them one heart [a new heart] and I will put a new spirit within them; and I will take the stony [unnaturally hardened] heart out of their flesh, and will give them a heart of flesh *[sensitive and responsive to the touch of their God]*" (Ezekiel 11:19, italics mine).

To be led by the Holy Spirit is a Joy Keeper that means you will live a righteous life, free from unfruitful works of the flesh. Don't allow the Joy Stealer to rob you by trying to run your own life. Let God anoint His plan for you by trusting Him.

In the next chapter, I'll show you how following a bunch of outward rules and regulations in an effort to keep yourself right with God is a Joy Stealer. And once you learn the next Joy Keeper, you won't have to tack up signs all over your house that say, "Don't Gossip. Don't Find Fault. Don't Be Critical. Don't Complain." God will write His laws on your heart, then you won't need reminders to keep your joy.

FOUR

Joy Stealer #2: Religious Legalism

⌒

The Lord says:

A new heart will I give you and a new spirit will I put
within you, and I will take away the stony heart out of
your flesh and give you a heart of flesh. And I will put
my Spirit within you and cause you to walk in My
statutes, *and you shall heed My ordinances and do them.*"
(Ezekiel 36:26–27, italics mine)

If you spend time acknowledging God and seeking His
plan for your life, He will cause you, by His Spirit, to walk
in obedience to His law and will lead you to joy. But your
joy will be stolen if you rely on following a strict set of rules
to feel righteous in the eyes of God.

Even the disciple Peter struggled to understand that we
are made righteous with God through faith alone, not
through following legalistic rules of religion. Peter fellow-
shipped freely with the Gentiles, but then separated himself
from them when religious men from Jerusalem arrived who

were preaching that Gentiles must be circumcised. Paul confronted Peter concerning this hypocrisy and wrote about it in his letter to the believers at Galatia:

> As soon as I saw that they were not straightforward and were not living up to the truth of the Gospel, I said to Cephas (Peter) before everybody present, If you, though born a Jew, can live [as you have been living] like a Gentile and not like a Jew, how do you dare now to urge and practically force the Gentiles to [comply with the ritual of Judaism and] live like Jews? [I went on to say] Although we ourselves (you and I) are Jews by birth and not Gentile (heathen) sinners, yet we know that a man is justified or reckoned righteous and in right standing with God not by works of the Law, but [only] through faith and [absolute] reliance on and adherence to and trust in Jesus Christ (the Messiah, the Anointed One). [Therefore] even we [ourselves] have believed on Christ Jesus, in order to be justified by faith in Christ and not by works of the Law [for we cannot be justified by any observance of the ritual of the Law given by Moses], because by keeping legal rituals and by works no human being can ever be justified (declared righteous and put in right standing with God). (Galatians 2:14–16)

Legalistic people, like the Pharisees of Jesus' day, are tied up in their own works instead of the work of Jesus. They have no joy; and they can't stand it if anyone else has joy. They are dried-up religious people who can't stand anything happy.

In fact, legalistic people think it is sinful to be happy. They believe it is wrong to laugh in church. To them, it is all right to get together and cry, but not to laugh and have fun.

Years ago, I was tied up in the legalistic bondage of my works instead of the work of Jesus, and that bondage prevented me from getting beyond myself. I was always examining myself, either condemning or approving based on my performance. It seemed to me that I couldn't do anything without feeling guilty. If I had any fun, I felt guilty. If I prayed, I felt guilty that I did not pray longer. If I was not working all the time, I felt guilty. I felt guilty every time I did not perfectly operate in the fruit of the Spirit.

Legalistic people bind themselves to unrealistic, religious laws of their own making. It is possible to make a law out of anything—even good things such as reading the Bible or praying. Discipline in these areas is good for us, but legalistic expectations should be avoided. We should *enjoy* God instead of just spending our lives struggling to be good enough to gain His approval.

The Pharisees operated in legalism; they took the joy out of everything, as we see in the following story of Jesus' healing of a man who was born blind:

As He passed along, He noticed a man blind from his birth. His disciples asked Him, Rabbi, who sinned, this man or his parents, that he should be born blind?

Jesus answered, It was not that this man or his parents sinned, but he was born blind in order that the workings of God should be manifested (displayed and illustrated) in him. We must work the works of Him Who sent Me and be busy with His business while it is daylight; night is coming on, when no man can work. As long as I am in the world, I am the world's Light.

When He had said this, He spat on the ground and made clay (mud) with His saliva, and He spread it [as ointment] on the man's eyes. And He said to him, Go, wash in the Pool of Siloam—which means Sent. So he went and washed, and came back seeing. (John 9:1–7)

This was a rather unusual method to treat blindness! Some people think it is strange to lay hands on a person and pray for them to be healed or to receive the fullness of the Holy Spirit.[1] What would they think of spitting as a way to minister to someone, as Jesus did in this verse?

But do you see how simple it was? The blind man did what Jesus said to do, even though His instructions seemed odd. The man probably thought, *What good will it do me to have mud rubbed on my eyes and go wash them in a dirty pool of water?* The point is the man came back seeing when he did as he was told.

Obeying the Lord's personal instructions is the catalyst to a miracle in many instances in the Bible. For example, in John chapter 2, some servants at a wedding obeyed the Lord and supernaturally received more wine to serve the guests. Jesus' mother had said to the servants, "Whatever He says to you, do it" (v. 5). So they filled some pots with water, as Jesus said, and Jesus performed His first miracle by turning the water into wine.

I believe if you and I will simply do what the Lord tells us to do in our hearts and in His Word, we, too, will receive a miracle breakthrough in our circumstances.

LEGALISM CAUSES TROUBLE

Being led only by rules of religion can keep people from seeing the miracles that God is performing every day, as the Pharisees were blinded to God's mercy in this story:

> When the neighbors and those who used to know him by sight as a beggar saw him, they said, Is not this the man who used to sit and beg? Some said, It is he. Others said, No, but he looks very much like him. But he said, Yes, I am the man.
>
> So they said to him, How were your eyes opened? He replied, The Man called Jesus made mud and smeared it on my eyes and said to me, Go to Siloam and wash. So I went and washed, and I obtained my sight!
>
> They asked him, Where is He? He said, I do not know. Then they conducted to the Pharisees the man who had formerly been blind.
>
> Now it was on the Sabbath day that Jesus mixed the mud and opened the man's eyes. (John 9:8–14)

The Pharisees were against Jesus even though He was sent from God and was doing good everywhere He went. They were governed by rules, laws, and customs, so they became upset when they learned Jesus had dared to heal this man on the Sabbath day. Up to that point, the Pharisees had not found anything with which to charge Jesus. But to them, the Sabbath was the wrong day to do any kind of work, even God's work.

Rules govern our own lives as well, in many areas, even in our spiritual experiences, and they can affect our lives positively or negatively. While laws are basically good, some people, like the Pharisees, get so caught up in religious legalism (the strict, literal adherence to the law) that they cannot really enjoy God or life.

There was a time when a person's relationship with God was based on a strict set of rules. In the Old Testament we read about a covenant of works called the Old Covenant. Under this covenant people had to follow the law. When they made mistakes, they had to make sacrifices to atone for them. There were so many laws that the people couldn't manage to keep them all.

But Jesus came and established a covenant of grace. Under this New Covenant, we have the wonderful gift of grace[2] because of Jesus' sacrifice on the cross. Our salvation and our relationship with Him are no longer based on keeping certain rules.[3] We can have a personal relationship with Jesus in which we don't have to struggle to do what is right. All we have to do is believe, depend on Him, and act on what He tells us to do.

LEGALISM MISSES MIRACLES

In the following verses, look at how legalism kept the Pharisees from simply receiving the awesomeness of the miracle Jesus had performed:

> So now again the Pharisees asked him how he received his sight. And he said to them, He smeared mud on my eyes, and I washed, and now I see. Then some of the Pharisees said, This Man [Jesus] is not from God,

because He does not observe the Sabbath. But others said, How can a man who is a sinner (a bad man) do such signs and miracles? So there was a difference of opinion among them.

Accordingly they said to the blind man again, What do you say about Him, seeing that He opened your eyes? And he said, He is [He must be] a prophet! However, the Jews did not believe that he had [really] been blind and that he had received his sight until they called (summoned) the parents of the man. (John 9:15–18)

Notice how the Pharisees had to dissect the miracle, take it apart, and try to reason it out? We will discuss reasoning later, but trying to figure out everything is a joy stealer that causes us to listen to our heads instead of our hearts.

Do you try to "figure out" everything that happens? Do you want to understand everything, to have all your ducks in a row? The Pharisees did. They were so caught up in reasoning and so busy dragging themselves around in the works of their own flesh, trying to obey the rules and keep the laws, they didn't have any time for joy or just resting in God and enjoying their lives. And they expected everyone else to do the same.

LEGALISM COMPLICATES EVERYTHING

The legalistic Pharisees focused on the broken rules instead of the joy of the blind man's deliverance:

They asked them, Is this your son, whom you reported as having been born blind? How then does he see now?

His parents answered, We know that this is our son, and that he was born blind. But as to how he can now see, we do not know; or who has opened his eyes, we do not know. He is of age. Ask him; let him speak for himself and give his own account of it. (John 9:19–21)

The man who had just been healed of lifelong blindness had to be feeling really happy. Their questions must have seemed to him like a bad joke. This whole cross-examination routine by the Pharisees must have been stealing his joy.

It is possible to make a law out of anything, and the Pharisees had bound themselves to unrealistic laws of their own making, which blinded them to the fact that Jesus was the Son of God. In a desperate attempt to prove otherwise, the Pharisees continued to question the man Jesus had healed.

As stated in *Matthew Henry's Commentary on the Whole Bible*, "One would have expected that such a miracle as Christ wrought upon the blind man would have settled his [Jesus'] reputation, and silenced and shamed all opposition, but it had the contrary effect; instead of being embraced as a prophet for it, he is prosecuted as a criminal."[4]

A legalistic, reasoning attitude complicates everything. It fills people with pride and blinds them to truth even when it is staring them right in the face, as this story illustrates:

His parents said this because they feared [the leaders of] the Jews; for the Jews had already agreed that if anyone should acknowledge Jesus to be the Christ, he should be expelled and excluded from the synagogue. On that account his parents said, He is of age; ask him.
So the second time they summoned the man who had been born blind, and said to him, Now give God

the glory (praise). This Fellow we know is only a sinner (a wicked person). Then he answered, I do not know whether He is a sinner and wicked or not. But one thing I do know, that whereas I was blind before, now I see. (John 9:22–25)

I cannot explain doctrinally everything the Lord has done in my life, any more than the blind man in this passage could explain his healing. I am not educated enough to use all the correct terminology in describing what has happened to me. But one thing I do know: Once I was a mess, and now I have been changed.

CHANGE THE WAY YOU THINK

Early in my Christian walk, I continually worked at trying to change things by myself. But many of the changes that have come about in my life began the day I finally realized that only God can make those changes.

That day I simply sat in the presence of God, weeping and telling Him, "If You don't change me, Lord, I am never going to be different because I have done everything anybody can do to change. I have tried everything I know. I have worked every formula. I have rebuked every devil. I have fasted. I have prayed. I have cried. I have begged and pleaded. And none of it has worked. So, Lord, either You will have to take me the way I am, or I will have to stay this way forever. If I am ever to be different, You have to change me. I give up."

When I finished talking, the Holy Spirit spoke in my heart, "Good. Now *I* can finally do something."

I had finally reached the point where I didn't care whether my ministry grew or not. I just wanted some peace. I had finally come to the place where I didn't care whether Dave or my children changed or not. I just wanted some peace. I had finally realized I would have to stop trying to change everything and everyone around me, including myself, and let God handle it if I was ever going to have peace.

You are never going to enjoy the promise of the new life[5] Jesus died to give you until you change the way you think. It's not about what you can do—it's about what Jesus has done for you.

Trying to face all the challenges of everyday life can cause you to get into human works, which rob you of your peace, joy, self-respect, and confidence. Works trap you into always struggling to *be* better so you will *feel* better about yourself. But if you try to do things on your own, you will be unable to bring about the positive changes you desire.

FREEDOM FROM LEGALISM

The following Scripture passage has an awesome message, confirming that only justification by faith, not works, releases joy in our lives:

> Therefore, since we are justified (acquitted, declared righteous, and given a right standing with God) through faith, let us [grasp the fact that we] have [the peace of reconciliation to hold and to enjoy] peace with God through our Lord Jesus Christ (the Messiah, the Anointed One). Through Him also we have [our] access (entrance, introduction) by faith into this grace

(state of God's favor) in which we [firmly and safely] stand. And let us rejoice and exult in our hope of experiencing and enjoying the glory of God. (Romans 5:1–2)

As children of God, we were never intended to live in legalistic bondage or any other kind of bondage. We should be experiencing glorious freedom and liberty—freedom to enjoy all God has given to us through His Son, Jesus.

But Satan tries to rob us of enjoying our lives. He accuses us, condemns us, and makes us feel insecure because he knows we cannot simultaneously enjoy life and have negative feelings about ourselves. Thank God, we can break out of his trap and start enjoying our blood-bought freedom and liberty.

We are told of our right to be free in Jesus in John 8:31–32, which says, "If ye continue in my word, then are ye my disciples indeed; and ye shall know the truth, and the truth shall make you free" (KJV); and again in verse 36: "If the Son therefore shall make you free, ye shall be free indeed" (KJV).

Are you enjoying spiritual freedom in Jesus or are you sacrificing your joy because you are trapped in the legalistic, rigid mind-set of believing you have to do it all? If you live a legalistic, rigid life, it will not be an enjoyable life. I know. The time came when I had to face the fact that I was legalistic and rigid, and although this truth was hard on me emotionally, God used it to set me free.

Jesus came that we might have and enjoy life to the fullest, until it overflows.[6] Following a narrow, legalistic lifestyle will lead us into works—futile efforts that will cause us to struggle and live in frustration. Remember, there is no bondage or burden in God. His rules (His ways for us to do things) are fulfilling and liberating.

Feeling guilty and condemned most of the time is not freedom. Being in mental and emotional turmoil is not freedom. Being sad and depressed is not freedom.

Have you reached the point where you are tired of trying to run the world? Are you willing to give up and ask God to help you? If so, pray this prayer:

Lord, I am tired of being legalistic and complicated. I just want to have some peace and enjoy my life. So, Lord, give me the desire to do what is right in Your eyes. If You don't do it, then it is not going to get done. I place my trust in You.

I encourage you to lay aside the limitations and defeat of legalism and do your best, beginning right now, to enjoy the life of freedom God has prearranged for us through Jesus. Instead of losing your joy over legalistic, self-made rules, the next Joy Keeper will show you how to find freedom to live in righteousness, peace, and joy[7] while God takes care of everything else.

FIVE

Joy Keeper #2: Be Free in Christ

The psalmist David wrote, "Behold, I long for Your precepts; in Your righteousness give me renewed life. . . . I will keep Your law continually, forever and ever [hearing, receiving, loving, and obeying it]. And I will walk at liberty and at ease, for I have sought and inquired for [and desperately required] Your precepts" (Psalm 119:40, 44–45).

If you truly love the Word of God—if you hear it, receive it, and *obey it*—you will have freedom and live "at ease." In other words, life will not be hard, frustrating, or difficult. Your joy is full when you believe God's promises for your life and obey *His* commands.

The Bible teaches that those who disobeyed God's instructions, who didn't listen to His Word did not enter into the place of rest He offered to them.[1] So when you feel frustrated or upset, or if you have lost your peace and your joy, ask yourself, "Am I believing God's Word?"

The only way we will ever be free from struggling is to believe the Word and obey whatever Jesus puts in our hearts to do. Believing God's Word delivers us from struggling so that we rest in the promises of God. The Word says, "For we who have believed (adhered to and trusted in and relied on God) do enter that rest" (Hebrews 4:3).

If your thoughts have become negative and you are full of doubt, it is because you have stopped hearing, receiving, and obeying God's Word. As soon as you start believing God's Word, your joy will return and you will be "at ease" again. And that place of rest in Him is where God wants you to be *every day* of your life.

THE LAW IS POWERLESS

The aim of God's law is to restrain the evil tendencies natural to man in his fallen state. But the law in itself is ineffective because it does not regulate humankind's behavior. In other words, the law does not have power to make people *want* to obey it.

Paul explained that we are made righteous with God simply *by believing* in Christ:

For no person will be justified (made righteous, acquitted, and judged acceptable) in His sight by observing the works prescribed by the Law. For [the real function of] the Law is to make men recognize and be conscious of sin [not mere perception, but an acquaintance with sin which works toward repentance, faith, and holy character]. But now the righteousness of God has been revealed independently and altogether apart from the Law, although actually it is attested by the Law and the Prophets, namely, the righteousness of God which comes by believing with personal trust and confident reliance on Jesus Christ (the Messiah). [And it is meant] for all who believe. For there is no distinction, since all have sinned and are falling short of the honor and glory which God bestows and receives. [All] are justified and made upright and in right standing with God, freely and gratuitously by His grace (His unmerited favor and mercy), through the redemption which is [provided] in Christ Jesus. (Romans 3:20–24)

As we read above, the real function of the law is to make us recognize our sin and realize our need of a Savior. The law only serves as a guideline to show us the righteousness of Christ, for He fulfilled all the law.

In fact, the law actually *increases* our inclination to sin. The Word says, "But then Law came in, [only] to expand and increase the trespass [making it more apparent and exciting opposition]" (Romans 5:20).

For example, suppose you have a tendency to eat too much chocolate. You want to be free from this habit, so you make a law for yourself: "I *must not* eat chocolate. I *cannot* eat chocolate. I *will never* eat chocolate again." You even convince yourself that for you it is a *sin* to eat chocolate.

This self-made law does not set you free from the desire for chocolate; it actually seems to increase your problem! Now all you can think about is chocolate. You want chocolate all the time. You have chocolate on your mind from daylight until dark.

Eventually, you find yourself sneaking around to eat chocolate because you told everybody you know that you are *never* going to eat chocolate again. You can't eat chocolate in front of people, so you hide when you eat your chocolate.

Now you feel really guilty because you have become a "sneaky" sinner.

If you know what I'm talking about, you know the pain that comes from being "under the Law" instead of free in Christ. Thank goodness it isn't a sin to eat chocolate, but if it were a sin and we confessed that sin to God, the Holy Spirit would give us the grace to lose our desire for it and we would enjoy freedom from that sin.

New believers who may be immature in their faith and weak in the knowledge of God's Word often focus their attention on God's laws in order to control their passions. But as they mature and learn to direct their attention to the leadership of the Holy Spirit, He will set them free from the *desire* to sin.

GRACE CHANGES OUR DESIRES

Paul explained that God's grace is the power to be delivered from temptation and evil. He wrote:

> But where sin increased and abounded, grace (God's unmerited favor) has surpassed it and increased the more and superabounded, so that, [just] as sin has reigned in death, [so] grace (His unearned and undeserved favor) might reign also through righteousness (right standing with God) which issues in eternal life through Jesus Christ (the Messiah, the Anointed One) our Lord. (Romans 5:20–21)

Remember, God gave the law so that we would realize what a mess we are without Him. The Word says, "If we say we have no sin [refusing to admit that we are sinners], we delude and lead ourselves astray, and the Truth [which the Gospel presents] is not in us [does not dwell in our hearts]" (1 John 1:8).

We all have sinned, but by grace God will empower us to lose the desire to continue sinning. He will cleanse us from the craving for it, as written here: "If we [freely] admit that we have sinned and confess our sins, He is faithful and just (true to His own nature and promises) and will forgive our sins [dismiss our lawlessness] and [continuously] cleanse us from all unrighteousness [everything not in conformity to His will in purpose, thought, and action]" (1 John 1:9).

It is hard to freely acknowledge we have sinned. But as verse 9 explains, if we will admit our sins to the Lord, He will cleanse us from everything that doesn't conform to His plan for us. Confessing our sins to God breaks their power over us and delivers us so that we can enjoy liberty in Christ every day of our lives.

I still remember the joy that hit my soul when I first began to understand this truth. First John 2:1 says, "My little children, I write you these things so that you may not violate God's law and sin. But if anyone should sin, we have an Advocate (One Who will intercede for us) with the Father—[it is] Jesus Christ [the all] righteous [upright, just, Who conforms to the Father's will in every purpose, thought, and action]." My paraphrase of what Paul was saying is, "I'm giving you this whole book so you may not sin, but if you do sin, don't get overwrought about it. Don't make a bigger deal out of it than what it has to be. Take your sin to Jesus. Admit your weaknesses. Admit you are human. Admit your imperfections."

When we confess our sins to God, He changes us from the inside out. He changes our desires so that we want what He wants. "So if the Son liberates you [makes you free men], then you are really and unquestionably free" (John 8:36).

There is a balance between disciplining ourselves and not coming under bondage to self-made laws. Obviously, God's commandments need to be followed. But when we follow a godly desire in our hearts to do the right thing, we no longer need to be led by the letter of the law. If Jesus is our Lord and Savior, obeying God is our hearts' desire and obedience brings us much joy. Many people still try to please God by obeying a list of rules of what to do or not do. But many of the rules they follow do not come from the Word of God, but from man-made religious rituals.

If we follow the leadership of the Holy Spirit, we will know exactly what we need to do to please God, because He will put a desire deep in our hearts to do what He would do.

What Laws Have You Made for Yourself?

Years ago, I turned cleaning my house into a law. I do believe we should have a clean house, and we ought to take care of what God gives us. But at that time in my life I was out of balance. In fact, I was overboard because a lot of my worth and value came from how things looked around me. I wanted my house to look absolutely perfect so no one would be able to find fault with me.

I cleaned my whole house from top to bottom every

single day of my life. I vacuumed, I dusted, I shined the mirrors, and I swept the floors.

One day, some of my friends were going somewhere and they invited me to go. I wanted to go with them, but my self-made law would not let me follow my heart. Then I resented my friends, who were out having a good time without me; I was even judgmental toward them. I wasn't free to follow the leadership of the Holy Spirit.

Life gets out of balance if we don't have *any* discipline. If we throw our work aside every time somebody wants us to do something different, we will never end up getting our houses cleaned. So we need to discipline ourselves with balance in order to take care of the things that need attention.

It is good to be disciplined, but it is not good to be legalistic. It was good for me to clean my house, but if somebody invited me to do something, and I had peace about it, then I needed to have the liberty to follow my heart. I needed to feel free enough to say, "This work can wait until tomorrow so that I can be with my friends."

I went through torment and agony over legalism. I was afraid to do almost anything. I was afraid to be free. I was afraid to follow the leadership of the Holy Ghost. I was afraid I would make a mistake and not hear from God. I felt safe when I followed rules and regulations; but I also felt condemned all the time.

The problem with the law is that it is perfect. The law is exactly what God would do—it is a picture of who He is—and what He wants us to do, too. Because the law is perfect, it is no wonder we can't keep it—because we are not perfect in our performance. There is no way we can ever follow all the prescribed rules and regulations of the law.

God did not give the law to us with the expectation that we could keep it. He gave the law to us to help us realize how much we need a Savior who can rescue us from our inability to keep His laws.

If we try to please God by obeying the law, we become proud when we are succeeding, but then we sin because we judge everyone who isn't keeping the law as we do. As soon as we realize our sin, we feel condemned again. We eventually learn there is no joy in following rules.

TRUST THE LEADERSHIP OF THE HOLY SPIRIT

Joy comes in following a heart that is made righteous by God. I remember when my desires started to change and line up with God's desire for me. At first I wondered what was wrong with me because I didn't want to do certain things anymore. Then I realized that God had changed my desires.

I once read that we believers are like ships that God wants to turn out to sea to sail wherever the wind and waves carry us. That sea represents the freedom we have in God, and the wind is a symbol of the Holy Spirit. But as new believers, we are tied to the dock because that is the only place we can avoid becoming shipwrecked until we learn how to follow Him. When we learn to follow those inner promptings of the Holy Spirit, we can be untied from the dock and sail the seas of life under His leadership without the fear of becoming lost.

God's leading doesn't contradict the laws that He ordained. When we are new believers, we learn to follow

God's laws that He defined in the Word, and as we mature we develop the ability to be led by the Spirit of the living God.

Paul explains:

> We [Jewish Christians] also, when we were minors, were kept like slaves under [the rules of the Hebrew ritual and subject to] the elementary teachings of a system of external observations and regulations. But when the proper time had fully come, God sent His Son, born of a woman, born subject to [the regulations of] the Law, to purchase the freedom of (to ransom, to redeem, to atone for) those who were subject to the Law, that we might be adopted and have sonship conferred upon us [and be recognized as God's sons]. And because you [really] are [His] sons, God has sent the [Holy] Spirit of His Son into our hearts, crying, Abba (Father)! Father! (Galatians 4:3–6)

When the Spirit of God is in you, the law of God is written in your heart. You no longer have to memorize the law because you can follow the leadership of the Holy Ghost, who will lead you in the right direction.

Some people feel much safer following the law than being led by the Spirit. They think they are okay as long as they follow a prescribed plan that everyone else is following. But following the Spirit may lead people to do something a little different from what everyone else is doing. They will need faith to leave the security of the crowd because God doesn't lead everybody to serve Him in exactly the same place or at the same capacity.

We cannot follow the leadership of the Holy Ghost by

simply obeying laws, rules, and regulations. The law is our tutor, but it is not to be our master. To live at ease and be full of joy, we must learn to prayerfully follow the Holy Spirit.

PRAY ABOUT EVERYTHING

I could not even begin to tell you now how much I pray during any given day. I really don't know. I just talk with God all through the day. I talk to Him when I'm doing my hair. I talk to Him in the middle of the night. I talk to Him about everything. I talk to Him about little things. I talk to Him about big things. And talking to Him always brings joy to my life.

I used to hear about different problems and situations in people's lives and determine that I would remember to pray for them. In a short time, I would accumulate a bunch of things that I needed to pray about. Now, as soon as I hear that someone has a need, I stop and pray right then.

Prayer needs to be like breathing—just a natural part of our lives. We are to be constantly in fellowship with God so He can lead us in the way that we should go. This is what Paul meant when he wrote, "Pray without ceasing" (1 Thessalonians 5:17 NKJV). This doesn't mean we are to go sit in the corner somewhere and not do anything but concentrate on a formalized program of prayer all day long. It means that we *live* a life of prayer.

One of the greatest signs of spiritual maturity is having the faith to step out and do what God is leading you to do, even if no one else seems to be doing it. Perhaps God led you to participate in a focus of ministry years ago, but now you are feeling a desire to reach out to a new area of service. God may have anointed you to lead a Bible study or to work at a certain place. There may have been a time when this was easy for you to do, but now it seems hard. God may be finished with what He sent you there to accomplish.

When what you are doing doesn't give you joy, when there is no life in it for you anymore, that is a strong indication that God is finished with whatever He was working through you.

Prayer will help you find out if God is leading you to make changes. When you think, *I'm laboring with this now. It doesn't minister to me anymore; there's no joy in it for me anymore*, then you should pray for God to lead you to where He wants you to be.

When God anoints your life, it is easy and filled with joy. Jesus said, "Take My yoke upon you and learn of Me, for I am gentle (meek) and humble (lowly) in heart, and you will find rest (relief and ease and refreshment and recreation and blessed quiet) for your souls. For My yoke is wholesome (useful, good—not harsh, hard, sharp, or pressing, but comfortable, gracious, and pleasant), and My burden is light and easy to be borne" (Matthew 11:29–30).

Some individuals don't have any joy because they are trying to do things God is not anointing them to do anymore. They are simply trying to ride a dead horse. The "horse" may have been dead for seven years, but they are still sitting there trying to get where it used to take them.

When the horse isn't moving, it is time to dismount!

Have the boldness and courage to say, "I did things a certain way for a long time, but this isn't the way God is leading me now. I believe God is leading me to do thus and so, and I'm going to follow the leadership of the Holy Spirit."

There Is Joy in Following God

We need to be free of traditional legalism and see what new things God wants us to do. People who feel condemnation because they can't obey the rules remain disappointed with themselves, and then they cannot enjoy their relationship with God.

I think most of us can relate to this prayer that someone shared with me: "Dear Lord, so far today, I've done all right. I haven't gossiped. I haven't lost my temper. I haven't been greedy, grumpy, nasty, selfish, or overindulgent; and God, I am really glad about that. But in a few minutes, God, I'm going to get out of bed, and from then on, I'm probably going to need a lot more help!"

I think many believers feel God is not happy with them—that God is mad at them and that they need to try harder to be acceptable to God. They want a list of things to do that will make them acceptable to God. At the end of the day, they want to receive little check marks for good behavior. If they can get a star on their chart and feel good about themselves, they will feel that God is happy with them.

But God doesn't want us living like that. He wants us to depend on Him and be led by the Holy Ghost. God's Word says clearly, "He has showed you, O man, what is good.

And what does the Lord require of you but to do justly, and to love kindness and mercy, and to humble yourself and walk humbly with your God?" (Micah 6:8).

He wants to lead us to do things that are good for us, like spending time with Him, but He doesn't want us to turn our devotional time into a law. As soon as we turn our desire to follow Him into a law, our whole relationship with God depends on obedience to that law instead of obedience to His voice and His Word.

If you are tired of trying to follow the rules to please God, and you are ready to trust God's grace to help you have joy every day of your life, I encourage you to admit your need of God's help by praying this prayer:

> *God, I want to do everything just the way Jesus would do it, but the sad fact is that it seems the more plans I make to be better, the worse I act. I can't do what is right without Your power. I need Your help. I want to be led by Your Spirit today. I want Your will to be done, not mine. I want to do whatever You want me to do.*

As your relationship with God matures, you will find yourself living less by guidelines, rules, and regulations, and more by the desires of your heart. As you learn more of the Word, you will find His desires fill your heart with joy. God wants you to know His heart well enough that you will want to follow the prompting, leading, and guidance of the Holy Spirit.

Once you are free in Christ, stand fast in that liberty and do not become ensnared with the Joy Stealer of legalism, which is the yoke of bondage that you have put off.[2] God wants to bring you into a new place that is full of freedom to follow your heart because that is where His law abides.

God will also give you variety and leadership because you will not want to abuse your freedom as you do what God wants you to do. Then He will cut you loose from the dock, and you can sail the ocean and start flowing in the joy of the Holy Ghost.

SIX

Joy Stealer #3:
Complicating Simple Issues

⁓

Having the tendency to complicate things is another thing that will steal your joy. Paul wrote, "But I fear, lest somehow, as the serpent deceived Eve by his craftiness, so your minds may be corrupted from the simplicity that is in Christ" (2 Corinthians 11:3 NKJV).

Learn to keep life as simple as possible. As I said before, it is fine to have a plan for your life and for your everyday activities, but be open to following God's plan if He has another direction in which He wants you to go.[1] We can actually veil or block God's plan by following our own fleshly desires and plans without consulting Him and striving to make ourselves acceptable to Him.

God's plan for us is actually so simple that many times we miss it. We tend to look for something more complicated— something more difficult, something we think we are expected to do to please God.

Jesus has told us what to do to begin to follow God's

plan: Believe![2] My life is an example of the magnitude of God's ability to fulfill His plan in our lives, no matter how unlikely the possibility may seem, when we simply believe.

"I Believe It"

I used to be such a complicated person. My way of seeing things and doing things was so complicated that it kept me from enjoying anything.

We say that we live in a complicated society, but I believe we are the complicated ones, and we complicate life. I don't think life is so complicated; I think it is our approach to life that is complicated. Serving God should not be complicated, and yet it can become very complicated and complex. I believe we are the ones who make it that way.

Think about the simple, uncomplicated approach a child has to life. Something that children seem to have in common is this: They are going to enjoy themselves if at all possible. They are carefree and completely without concern. And they believe what they are told. It is their nature to trust unless they have had an experience in that area that taught them otherwise.

Jesus wants us to grow and mature in our behavior, but He also wants us to remain childlike with an attitude of trust and dependence toward Him.[3] Remember, He told us in John 3:16, "God so loved the world that He gave His only begotten Son, that whoever *believes* in Him should not perish but have everlasting life" (NKJV, italics mine). All He wants to hear us say is "I believe it."

Believing simplifies life. It releases joy and leaves us free to enjoy our lives while God takes care of our circumstances.

As we saw earlier, God told Abraham a wild story about giving him a baby when he was a hundred years old and his wife was past the age of childbearing. Abraham didn't complicate matters by trying to figure it all out. He simply *believed* God. In fact, he believed so strongly that he laughed—it was fun; he enjoyed it.

That is what you have to start doing if you want to have any joy. Simply believe God.

When God says something to you in your heart, or when you read something in the Bible, you should say: "I believe it. If God says that He will prosper me, I believe it.[4] If He says that I will reap if I give,[5] I believe it. If He says to forgive my enemies,[6] even though it doesn't make any sense to me, I believe it—and, instead of going to beat them up, I am going to do what He says. If He says to pray for my enemies,[7] I believe it, and I am going to do it. If He says to call 'things that are not as though they were,'[8] I believe it, and I am going to do it."

DO THINGS GOD'S WAY

What Jesus told Peter to do in this next passage probably didn't make any sense to him in the natural. But Peter simply did what the Lord said, and he received what was probably the biggest catch of his fishing career:

> When He had stopped speaking, He said to Simon, "Launch out into the deep and let down your nets for a catch."

But Simon answered and said to Him, "Master, we have toiled all night and caught nothing; *nevertheless at Your word* I will let down the net."

And when they had done this, they caught a great number of fish, and their net was breaking. (Luke 5:4–6 NKJV, italics mine)

Once you get over the hump of living in the natural realm and being led by your thoughts, feelings, and emotions, you can make the transition of getting to the place where you just start doing what the Lord says.

Remember, in John chapter 9 Jesus said to the man who was born blind, "Let me put this mud on your eyes. Then go wash in the pool of Siloam." The man did, and he came back seeing. It is amazing what God will do for you if you simply do what He tells you to do.

I believe God has a plan for your breakthrough—but you have to trust Him. You have to believe. You have to do things His way whether it makes any sense to you or not.

KEEP IT SIMPLE

Have you ever invited people to your home and then didn't enjoy their visit? Why? Was it because, like the following illustration of Martha, you turned that simple time of fellowship into something it should not have been?

Jesus entered a certain village, and a woman named Martha received and welcomed Him into her house. And she had a sister named Mary, who seated herself at the Lord's feet and was listening to His teaching.

But Martha [overly occupied and too busy] was distracted with much serving; and she came up to Him and said, Lord, is it nothing to You that my sister has left me to serve alone? Tell her then to help me [to lend a hand and do her part along with me]!

But the Lord replied to her by saying, Martha, Martha, you are anxious and troubled about many things; there is need of only one or but a few things. Mary has chosen the good portion [that which is to her advantage], which shall not be taken away from her. (Luke 10:38–42)

Most of us occasionally like to invite a few people over for fellowship. But if we are going to have somebody over to our house, we ought to enjoy it.

I have noticed that complicated people like me, and like Martha in this passage, get burned out easily because we tend to make everything so much harder than it ought to be. Let me give you a personal example.

In the earlier days of my life, I might have said to a group of friends, "Why don't you come over next Sunday after church? We'll throw some hot dogs on the grill, open up some potato chips and some pork and beans, I'll make some tea, and we'll have some good fellowship."

They would have said, "Okay. We'll come; that sounds like fun."

Well, that felt good to me. It seemed to be easy and something I could do without a lot of fuss and bother.

But I just couldn't leave it alone. The hot dogs became steaks, and the potato chips became potato salad. I had invited six people, but then I started thinking about the twelve I didn't invite who might get upset if they knew the six were coming, and everything quickly got out of hand.

Now we had eighteen people coming over. We had to buy lawn furniture, which we couldn't afford, paint the barbecue pit, wax all the floors, cut the grass, and plant new flowers.

All of a sudden a simple barbecue with friends had turned into a nightmare—all because I had the "Martha syndrome." I had "Martha" written all over me. That is what I meant earlier when I said that I couldn't enjoy life because I was too complicated. Eventually, I became angry with everyone in the house because I had to work so hard trying to prepare for the party. Soon I started feeling resentful and thinking, *I don't know why these people have to come to our house anyway.*

Then Saturday came, and Dave wanted to go play golf. So I got mad at him because he wanted to play golf while I had to stay home and do all the work for this big party we were having the next day.

Why couldn't I just keep it simple? I had an ungodly need to impress everyone. I did have a problem, but it was one that *I* had created. I needed to learn to be more like Mary and less like Martha. Instead of worrying and fretting, I needed to learn to simplify my plans, lighten up, and enjoy life!

May I share something with you with all the love I know how to muster? If you are having problems in your life, it may be because you are creating many of them yourself. You may be taking things that could be simple, fun, easy, and even inexpensive, and making a big deal out of them. Then you probably get mad at everyone around you because you are frustrated. You are frustrated because you aren't sticking with what was in your heart to start with; instead, you have started complicating it.

Living a complicated lifestyle will steal your joy. Simplicity will bring power and peace.

It may be difficult to do, but you can learn to have a simple approach to everything. It begins by accepting the simplicity that is yours in Christ Jesus. That means giving up struggling and striving and simply leaning on and depending on Him. The next Joy Keeper will show you how being uncomplicated simply means trusting God. Trust releases both peace and joy, as well as the blessings of God,[9] and it is the key to enjoying every single day of your life.

SEVEN

Joy Keeper #3: Be Uncomplicated

∽

Do you feel that your life is still too complicated? I believe Satan works hard to complicate your life so he can steal your joy, but God wants you to love and enjoy your life. I want to share a few more principles that can open the door to new levels of joy for you every day.

Jesus said, "I am the Door; anyone who enters in through Me will be saved (will live). He will come in and he will go out [freely], and will find pasture. The thief comes only in order to steal and kill and destroy. I came that they may have and enjoy life, and have it in abundance (to the full, till it overflows)" (John 10:9–10).

I believe we need to make every effort to simply enjoy Jesus every single day that God gives us. If we trust in Him, joy should be radically abundant and overflowing in our lives.

DON'T WORRY ABOUT WHAT OTHERS THINK

Years ago, I realized I wasn't enjoying my work because I worried over what others thought about my ministry. Finally I made up my mind that if I was going to give every day of my life to preaching the gospel, I was going to enjoy it. I realized I couldn't enjoy the meetings if I was concerned about what everybody thought about me. I couldn't enjoy my work if I tried to keep everyone happy.

I have to be free from the entanglement of complicated thoughts. I simply have to stay focused on what God has anointed me to do.

You have to be free, too, if you are going to enjoy your life. You will never find joy if you don't understand the power of simplicity.

I believe Satan works overtime to complicate everything he can that involves us. He wants to distract us with confusion and complications so we cannot enjoy God's blessings. Satan doesn't want you to enjoy anything, even a simple barbeque with friends, so he'll move in and try to make sure you work yourself so hard you will never want to invite guests to your home for dinner again.

People do the same thing at holidays. They get into major debt trying to buy presents because they are afraid of what people will think if they don't give them gifts. If you really don't have the money, just tell people you can't afford to buy presents this year. Truth is simple.

Life gets complicated when we try to ignore or hide the truth. And the majority of people do not get angry with others for being honest and telling the truth. There may be a few people who are offended. There may even be some who believe you should go into debt just to buy them something they don't even need to start with. But people like that are going to get mad at you for something anyway, so you might as well simplify your life and be truthful.

DON'T ACCUMULATE TOO MANY THINGS

Do you have any idea how many things we think we have to own just to be reasonably happy compared to what it *really* takes to live? Dave and I have had to spend so much of our time living in hotel rooms while traveling with our ministry, I've learned to fit everything I really need in a few suitcases. Although some people tease me about taking a lot of stuff, I leave a lot at home, which means I can live without it. It's amazing how little we really do need. While there are a lot of things in my home I thought I couldn't live without, I don't have any of those things 60 percent of the time because I'm on the road—and I do just fine without them.

Some of us have so much that we can hardly walk through our houses. When I first realized my need to find simplicity, I became acutely aware that every knickknack I was tempted to buy would soon be just one more thing I would have to dust at home.

Simplify your home. Don't have so much stuff all over the place that you feel confused when you walk in the door and say, "How can anybody live in this mess?" If you find yourself complaining about the way you live, start doing something about it. You can have life-changing joy if you simplify your everyday life.

Some people even complicate going out for dinner because they can't decide where to go. Don't create confusion over what restaurant to eat at. Avoid the "Should we go here? Should we go there?" syndrome. I myself could really complicate this decision if I weren't careful because I like the coffee at one place, the salad at another, and the pasta at still another! And some days I would really like to have it all, but I have to just pick a place and go.

Indecisiveness makes life complicated. Learn to make decisions about simple activities. Just do *something*. Make a decision and go joyfully about your business.

This part of the book may not be deep, but learning to apply simplicity to your life is powerful. In fact, while you are teaching yourself new habits, ask God to remind you to take a simple approach to life.

DON'T TRY TO DO TOO MUCH

If you want to live a less complicated life, you may have to simplify it by not doing so much. Most people who are stressed and frustrated have become burned out because they try to squeeze too much into their schedules.

I used to whine, grumble, and murmur about my schedule, saying, "How can anybody do all this? I never have any time to rest. I never take a vacation." God finally told me one day, "You're making the schedule. Nobody is making you do all that. If you don't want to do it all, then just don't do some of it."

If you don't want to do everything you have scheduled, I suggest that you take an hour or so and write down everything you are doing or want to do. Then look at which events are not bearing any fruit and mark them off your list. More than likely you will find several activities that are not productive in your life because God was done with that assignment for you a long time ago. And because you are still doing it, perhaps you never have time for other things such as praying and spending time with God.

Don't include so many things in your schedule that your life feels like a confused mess because you're going nonstop from one commitment to another. Do something about it. You are too busy if you never have time to rest. You are too busy if you never have time to laugh or have any fun.

God told me, "You're the only one who can do anything about being too busy. I'm not making you do all that stuff."

So learn to say no to a few things. Practice saying it: "No!" It's a simple word that becomes easier to say with each use.

Learn to say yes to what is really important. Don't be like Martha and become anxious and troubled about many things. Choose the better part of life, and take time to enjoy important moments in life.

Before I uncomplicated my life, I never had time to enjoy my home. I never enjoyed my kids. I loved them, but I never really took time to *enjoy* them. I was too busy doing other things that seemed more important at the time than playing with my kids.

Spend time with your family. Spend time with your spouse, your children, and your grandkids. Spend time with friends. Enjoy God. Many people are too busy even to take a walk. Take a little bit of time to look at some of the things He's created.

Learning how to simplify your life is possibly one of the most important principles to understand, because Satan wants to steal your time. He steals your joy by making you too busy to enjoy all God has given you. Take time to laugh. Take time to enjoy your life.

SIMPLY TRUST GOD

Don't complicate your life by trying to understand what is wrong with your friends and family members who don't agree with you about everything. After many years of marriage, I still don't have Dave figured out. But I found joy when I simply quit trying to understand why he likes to watch sports and play golf so much.

You can't really love people until you quit trying to rework them and find joy in who they are. My life got real simple when I finally realized I couldn't change Dave.

God can change someone if He wants to, and if He doesn't, it's because He doesn't want to. So I might as well trust God. Trust is simple. Casting your care on Him is simple.

The Bible message is simple: Love God and love others.

The gospel is simple: Jesus loves us, this we know. Why? Because the Bible tells us so.

Even the plan of salvation is simple: Jesus died for us. He paid the price for our sin. How much simpler can it be?

It is amazing how a straightforward, uncomplicated message can change your life and bring joy.

The Bible says in 1 Corinthians 1:21 that God *chose* to change the world through the foolishness of preaching.[1] The word *foolishness* used in that verse is defined in *Strong's Exhaustive Concordance* as "silliness, i.e. absurdity." Sometimes it seems absurd that God has made it possible for us to preach to two-thirds of the world every day when He could have chosen many other ways to reveal His plan of salvation. But He *chose* to anoint the *simple* preaching of His Word to get people saved and set free from lifelong bondages.

The believers in Corinth tried to complicate the gospel just as people do today. Second Corinthians 11:3 says, "But I fear, lest by any means, as the serpent beguiled Eve through his subtilty, so your minds should be corrupted from the simplicity that is in Christ" (KJV).

In essence Paul said, "I'm afraid that if you're not very careful, Satan is going to deceive you and your mind will be corrupted and you will lose the simplicity that is your inheritance in Christ Jesus."

Jesus came to simplify your life. Satan wants to complicate your life, but God is not the author of confusion. The Amplified Bible translates Paul's concern this way: "But [now] I am fearful, lest that even as the serpent beguiled Eve by his cunning, so your minds may be corrupted and seduced from wholehearted and sincere and pure devotion to Christ" (2 Corinthians 11:3).

There are so many people in the church who are not really serving God with their whole hearts or their whole lives. Their lives are a big, complicated mess because they have one foot in the kingdom and one foot in the world.

There is nothing simpler than being wholeheartedly single-minded in your relationship with God. If you try to follow a double lifestyle, if you try to be "open-minded" for one group of friends and religious for your church friends, you will soon feel ripped apart because you are being double-minded; you are going in two different directions. The Bible says to serve God single-mindedly. That means you can say, "I serve God with my whole heart. This is the one thing I do, I live to serve Christ."

We went on a missions trip with a missionary friend of ours years ago, and when we got back he said, "Do you realize on that whole trip, you never talked about anything but Jesus and the Word?"

I said, "No, I didn't realize that, but I don't apologize." I'm so busy preaching the gospel, I'm not even aware that it is all I talk about most of the time. All of our family works at the ministry and we find it difficult to not talk about ministry-related issues when we get together. We love what we do and we are wholeheartedly committed to it.

I'm not saying it is wrong to talk about other things if they are good things. But I'm trying to make a point that life is sweet if we simply serve God.

God is not some sideline. God is the main line. A lot of people want to sideline their commitment to serve God and find a main line to His blessings. We need to jump into serving God with both feet. We mustn't live worldly half the time and godly the other half. We shouldn't go to work and laugh at dirty jokes, gossip about the boss, and hang around with people who are corrupting us. We must make up our minds to serve God with our whole hearts.

Wholehearted people can live a simple life because they are going in only one direction—toward God.

KEEP YOUR FAITH SIMPLE

In the Old Testament, the Israelites often said, "The Lord our God is one Lord [the only Lord]" (Deuteronomy 6:4).[2] And I always wondered why they made such a big deal out of God being One.

Then I realized that the heathens were deceived into believing there was a god for everything. Can you imagine how complicated that must have been? To have a baby, they talked to the god of fertility. To grow crops, they talked to the god of the harvest. And all these different gods required different sacrifices for healing, peace, or whatever the people lacked.

They must have been busy just running around to false gods. That's why it was such good news when the one true God revealed Himself and said, "I've got it all. Anything you need, you can come to Me."

The Lord our God is One.

The word *simple* means "one": "unmixed," "free of secondary complications."[3] The word *pure* also means "one": "unmixed with any other matter."[4]

Whatever I need, I can go to the one pure God. If I need peace, if I need righteousness, if I need hope, if I need joy, if I need healing, if I need finances, if I need help—whatever I need, I simply go to the one true God. That is simple. That delivers me from complication. The Lord our God, He is One.

Jesus' message that He came so we might have and enjoy our lives so abundantly they would overflow was intended for us in the twenty-first century. God did not mean for life to be as complicated as it is today. As Paul said, "I'm concerned for you, that you are going to lose the simplicity of Christ." We simply need to know who we are in Christ. We need to know that God has an individual plan for each one of us.

I believe Satan uses the spirit of religion against the church more than anything else to try to shut down the power of God. Religion teaches you to juggle the many tasks of Bible reading, prayer, confessing the Word, fasting, memorizing spiritual songs, and doing good deeds. Just when you think you are doing all right, the devil throws you a new requirement to work into your routine.

Decide not to live like that anymore. I tried to do all the things I thought I had to do to keep God happy, but God wasn't asking me to do most of it. I was just following other people; I thought I should do what they were doing because they were being blessed. Following people instead of God is another tool the devil uses to distract us from God's simple plan for our lives. I lived under the tyranny of self-inflicted "oughts and shoulds."

A religious spirit brings legalism instead of freedom. Religion is only about what *we can do*; Christianity is about what *Jesus has done*. Life gets complicated when we think we always have to do something.

"What can I do? What can I do?"

And people say that to God all the time. "What do You want me to *do*, God? What do You want me to do?"

He wants you to believe in what Jesus has already done.

Yet the devil will continue to scream in your ear, "Well, what are you going to do? What are you going to do?" We can stay so busy trying to think of ways to keep God happy that we never enjoy the lives He gave us.

JUST ASK GOD

Just pray and ask God, "How can I simplify my life? What am I doing, God, that's making life so complicated?"

Stop blaming everything on the devil and take a little bit of responsibility for your life. God will show you some ways to simplify your life, but then you have to be willing to follow through. Ask God to show you the areas of your life you may be complicating that should be simple; then return to simplicity.

One morning I was trying to get dressed, and even though God has blessed me with a lot of nice clothes, I had one of those days that nothing seemed "right." I would pick up an outfit and then put it back. Then I would get something else and put it back. I would hold it up in front of the mirror and want to start over. It was starting to frustrate me.

Then the Holy Spirit said, "Joyce, keep it simple. Just put something on your body and go."

We can get in such a habit of complicating life that we can't even get dressed without divine intervention! Ask God to reveal areas of indecision that may be complicating your life, then use this Joy Keeper of being uncomplicated to simplify your life.

KEEP YOUR PRAYERS SIMPLE

When I say "simplify" your prayer life, I don't mean that you should not pray often. The Bible says, "Pray without ceasing" (1 Thessalonians 5:17 NKJV). You need to pray frequently, and you need to pray as long as the anointing is on you to pray.

What I mean is that you can complicate your prayer life to the point of being unbearable if you try to sound too eloquent. Don't try to impress God. Just talk to Him like a friend; tell Him the way it is. Be sincere and be real. Don't put on religious airs. He knows what you need before you even ask Him.[5]

James taught that we don't have what we desire because we aren't asking God for it:

You are jealous and covet [what others have] and your desires go unfulfilled; [so] you become murderers. [To hate is to murder as far as your hearts are concerned.] You burn with envy and anger and are not able to obtain [the gratification, the contentment, and the happiness that you seek], so you fight and war. You do not have, because you do not ask. (James 4:2)

Jesus taught us that to be full of joy is simple. He said, "Ask and keep on asking and you will receive, so that your joy (gladness, delight) may be full and complete" (John 16:24). If you want joy in your life, simply ask God for it.

EIGHT

Joy Stealer #4: Excessive Reasoning

~

Along with works of the flesh, legalism, and being over-complicated, excessive reasoning is another thing that steals our joy. Reasoning occurs when we try to figure out the "why" or "how" behind something. When we reason excessively, our minds revolve around and around a problem as we try to understand it, which causes a whirlwind of worry and confusion.

If you want to have joy, you must stop trying to figure out everything. You must stop rolling your problems around in your mind. You have to quit anxiously searching for an answer to your situation, trying to find out what you should do about it.

I remember one night Dave and I had an argument. Dave is easygoing and gets over things quickly, but even after our disagreement is settled, I always have to try to figure out why we argued in the first place. I am the kind of person who wants to know "why" things happen the way they do.

If you are like I was, you will not enjoy your life because there are too many things you will never figure out. You have to be able to simply let things go. God knows why things happen, but you don't have to know. You can decide to move on without knowing the details. If God wants to tell you, He will tell you. But don't drive yourself crazy trying to figure it out.

That night, after Dave and I argued, it was over as far as he was concerned. We kissed and made up, and Dave went to bed and fell asleep. But I went into my office to "figure it out."

I was determined to understand why we argued. I prayed, "God, I've got to understand what happens when we do this, because I don't want this to happen anymore. And I'm going to figure this out. Why, God, why? What did I do wrong? What did he do wrong? Why does this have to happen?"

I was just getting more frustrated. I was not hearing from God. I wasn't getting any answers. I was working myself into a fit of frustration, and I finally cried, "God, what am I going to do? What am I going to do?"

And the Holy Spirit said to me, "Why don't you just try going to bed?" God was showing me how to avoid excessive reasoning in my life.

When Jesus saw that His disciples were trying to "figure out" what to do about the fact they had forgotten to bring bread to feed the crowd, He said to them, "O ye of little faith, why reason ye among yourselves?" (Matthew 16:8 KJV).

I spent many years attempting to solve my own problems and finally discovered that it is not God's will for me to do that. All my efforts did was make me frustrated and more selfish and self-centered. I focused on myself and expected everyone else to focus on me, too. I looked to others to do for me what only God could do.

Psalm 37:3 contains a wonderful secret for problem solving: "Trust in the LORD and do good" (NIV). Doing good for others is a seed we can sow, and trusting God is the way we receive our harvest from that sown seed.[1]

Another thing the Bible tells us to do when we have a problem is to *cheer up*.[2] In John 16:33, Jesus says: "I have told you these things, so that in Me you may have [perfect] peace and confidence. In the world you have tribulation and trials and distress and frustration; *but be of good cheer* [take courage; be confident, certain, undaunted]! For I have overcome the world. [I have deprived it of power to harm you and have conquered it for you.]" (italics mine).

We go around figuring and reasoning and asking, "Why, God, why?" and "When, God, when?" because we want to know now so we won't have to trust God. We don't want any surprises; we want to be in control because we are afraid things won't turn out the way we want. This driving desire to be "in the know" will usually produce one thing—a mind riddled with over-reasoning.

"Why, God, why?" and "When, God, when?" are two statements that can keep us frustrated and prevent us from enjoying the lives Jesus died to give us. Many times we do not understand what God is doing, but that is what trust is all about. Nobody says we have to know everything; no one has ever told us we have to understand everything. We need to be satisfied in knowing the One who does know and understand. We need to learn to trust God, not ourselves.

ARE YOU TRUSTING OR WORRYING?

Many times we say we are trusting God, but our minds are worrying. As the following verses confirm, we are to trust the Lord not only with our hearts but also with our minds:

> Lean on, trust in, and be confident in the Lord with all your heart and mind and do not rely on your own insight or understanding. In all your ways know, recognize, and acknowledge Him, and He will direct and make straight and plain your paths. (Proverbs 3:5–6)

What do you let your mind do when you have problems? Do you try to figure things out instead of leaving them in God's capable hands?

There is the mind of the flesh, which is wrong thinking based on your thoughts and reasoning. And there is the mind of the Spirit,[3] which is right thinking based on the Word of God and the inner promptings of the Holy Spirit. Confusion, frustration, and anxiety are the products of operating in the mind of the flesh. Joy is the product of the Spirit and of following the leading of the Spirit in prayer and fellowship with God.

If you operate in the mind of the Spirit, you can have "the peace of God, which passeth all understanding,"[4] and you can have "joy unspeakable" and be "full of glory"[5] right in the middle of terrible trials and tribulations.

The peace *which passeth all understanding* and *joy unspeakable* are types of peace and joy that don't make any sense. In other words, when you have these types of peace and joy within, you are happy without having any particular reason to be happy. You are happy just because you know that God is and that He is able to *direct and make straight and plain your paths* in an exceedingly, abundantly above-all-you-can-ask-or-think way.[6]

You don't have to try to change yourself or anyone else—and that makes you happy. You don't have to worry about tomorrow—and that makes you happy. You don't have to worry about yesterday—and that makes you happy. You don't have to know how to do everything—and that makes you happy.

All you need to do is know the One who knows.

Trying to figure things out will only wear you out. But if you trust God for the answers, you can enter His rest.

REST YOUR MIND

This Scripture contains the key to having joy in your life every day: "Be not wise in your own eyes; reverently fear and worship the Lord and turn [entirely] away from evil. It shall be health to your nerves and sinews, and marrow and moistening to your bones" (Proverbs 3:7–8).

You have to lay aside trying to figure out everything and quit being wise in your own eyes. Remember, too, that in all your ways you must acknowledge the Lord, trusting Him to direct your paths. No one is smart enough to figure out everything in this life. Thank God, we don't have to. All we have to do is turn entirely away from evil, and it will be health to our nerves. This turning involves making correct choices in obedience to God's Word.

Are you saying, "I'm nervous; I need some counseling?" What you really need may be simply to stop reasoning and start resting. Just think about how much your life would change if you would let your mind rest.

I am learning not to worry, but I do have a lot of things to take care of, so I sometimes find myself thinking too much. When that happens I try to take a break so my mind can be still. One of my favorite things to do in the evening is to just sit down for a couple of hours and watch a good film or an old movie from the forties or fifties— something I know is going to be clean. The reason I like to do that so much is because the reasoning part of my mind can just shut down. I also like to look through magazines or catalogs. It helps me get my mind off everything else.

It is good for us to do things that give our minds a rest now and then.

If your mind is going all the time, constantly trying to figure out something, you need to let the Holy Spirit work with you to quiet your mind. If you have a problem you can't solve, instead of all that reasoning, just stop and pray: "Lord, I can't figure this out. I don't have the answer. I don't know what to do. I don't understand what You are doing in this situation, but I am going to trust You."

That is what God's people did when they realized they were helpless against their enemies and they couldn't figure out what to do. Their king prayed to God: "For we have no might to stand against this great company that is coming against us. We do not know what to do, but our eyes are upon You" (2 Chronicles 20:12).

Later, in verse 17, the Lord says to them, "You shall not need to fight in this battle; take your positions, *stand still*, and see the deliverance of the Lord" (italics mine).

You have only two options in life. You can try to do everything yourself, or you can let God do it for you. If you are going to let God do it for you, you don't have to camp on top of it mentally all the time, trying to dissect it and figure it out.

We saw in the passage of Proverbs 3:7–8 that allowing God to have total control of our lives has a positive effect on our health. I think that passage is talking about our entire health. Leaning on God instead of trying to reason and figure out everything will make us healthier—in spirit, soul, and body.

LEAN ON GOD

Jesus tells us in the following verses that we are to be fruitful, but He also tells us that apart from Him we can do nothing to produce that fruit. Notice that He doesn't say anything about fruitfulness being dependent on human knowledge.

> Dwell in Me, and I will dwell in you. [Live in Me, and I will live in you.] Just as no branch can bear fruit of itself without abiding in (being vitally united to) the vine, neither can you bear fruit unless you abide in Me. I am the Vine; you are the branches. Whoever lives in Me and I in him bears much (abundant) fruit. However, apart from Me [cut off from vital union with Me] you can do nothing. (John 15:4–5)

The apostle Paul was a smart man who possessed a lot of knowledge. He was a Pharisee of Pharisees, learned, educated. And before he was converted on the road to Damascus,[7] he was very proud of what he knew.

Isn't it interesting that sometimes the more people know, the more proud they become?

In 1 Corinthians 8:1, Paul said that knowledge puffs up, but charity (love) edifies (or builds up). If we knew everything we think we would like to know, we wouldn't lean on God because we would be so proud we would think we didn't need Him.

Remember, the Lord told us, "Apart from Me . . . you can do nothing." He could have put it this way: "Apart from Me, I am not going to let you do anything." Our God is a jealous God.[8] He wants to be first in our lives. He wants us to lean on Him. He wants us to need Him. That is why He created us with some weaknesses and not just strengths. He knew that if we had no weaknesses or inabilities, if we never failed at all, we would never need to go to Him for anything.

We will never be entirely "fixed up" because if we are, we won't need God.

I am desperate for God. I know if God doesn't come through for me, I cannot do anything that makes any sense or has any value.

Psalm 127:1 says, "Except the Lord builds the house, they labor in vain who build it." Notice it does not say that they *can't* build it. It says that it will be built *in vain*, meaning it will never do those who build it any good. It will never amount to anything. It will never produce the desired joy and peace. According to *Barnes' Notes*, verse 1 refers to placing our "entire dependence on God for success"⁹ in whatever we do.

Even if I had been able to successfully build my own ministry—which I wasn't, thank God—He would not have allowed it to be truly built. It would never have really blessed anyone or done anyone any real good.

The bottom line is: *If God is not in it, it is not going to work.*

Paul came full circle from thinking he knew everything to saying in this next verse that he had resolved to know nothing but Jesus Christ and Him crucified: "For I resolved to know nothing (to be acquainted with nothing, to make a display of the knowledge of nothing, and to be conscious of nothing) among you except Jesus Christ (the Messiah) and Him crucified" (1 Corinthians 2:2). I believe Paul was saying, "All I know is Jesus. He died for me, was raised from the dead, and is in control. He is in charge; I'm not. He is on my side, and I don't have to know anything more than that."

Think about how much frustration you would save yourself if you just gave up worrying and trying to figure everything out and were resolved to know nothing but Jesus, as Paul was.

ARE YOU PONDERING OR WORRYING?

At this point you may be saying, "But we are not supposed to be ignorant, never knowing what is going on."

I agree. As we see in this passage, when the angel came and appeared to Mary and spoke to her about conceiving and giving birth to the promised Messiah, she pondered, or thought about, those things:

> The angel said to her, Do not be afraid, Mary, for you have found grace (free, spontaneous, absolute favor and loving-kindness) with God. And listen! You will become pregnant and will give birth to a Son, and you shall call His name Jesus. He will be great (eminent) and will be called the Son of the Most High; and the Lord God will give to Him the throne of His fore-father David, and He will reign over the house of Jacob throughout the ages; and of His reign there will be no end. . . .
>
> Then Mary said, Behold, I am the handmaiden of the Lord; let it be done to me according to what you have said. And the angel left her. . . . But Mary was keeping within herself all these things (sayings), weighing and pondering them in her heart. (Luke 1:30–33, 38; 2:19)

As Jesus grew up, although Mary knew what the Lord had told her about His being the Savior of His people, she didn't really understand it all—just as Jesus' disciples didn't understand everything He taught them.[10]

I don't believe there is anything wrong with pondering some things in our hearts as Mary did. Many times it is while we are pondering or meditating on something that God gives us revelation or understanding. But it is one thing to ponder; it is another thing to worry.

I think that when we are pondering, in a sense we are praying. We are saying, "Lord, I don't know what this means. I don't really understand it. I need some direction." That is different from sitting around trying to figure it out.

93

You may wonder, *How can I tell when I cross over the line?*

As soon as you become confused, you have left off pondering and gone into excessive reasoning. That is a very good indicator to remember. It is one that God taught me.

CONFUSION IS NOT FROM GOD

I was holding a meeting in Kansas City, and it came to my heart to ask the audience how many of them were confused. There were about 300 people at that meeting, and from what I could tell, 298 of them raised their hands. And my husband was one of the two who didn't raise a hand.

I can tell you that Dave has never been confused in his life because he doesn't worry. He doesn't try to figure out anything. He is not interested in having all the answers to everything because he trusts God.

When you trust God, you can relax and enjoy life. "For God is not the author of confusion, but of peace" (1 Corinthians 14:33 KJV). You don't have to go through life worrying and trying to figure out how to solve all your problems.

Think about all the things you have worried about in your life and how they have all worked out. That ought to help you realize that worry and reasoning are a waste of time and energy.

I have four grown children. It amazes me when I look back at everything I went through with them as they were growing up—when they didn't get good grades in school, when I was called to the principal's office because of them, when the neighbor complained about them, when it looked as if they would never want to work or do anything worthwhile or would never be able to handle their finances.

I would think, *How are they ever going to handle life when they get away from me? They can't even handle their allowance.*

One of my daughters couldn't keep anything clean and could never find anything. Laura would walk into the house and immediately drop her coat, her shoes, and her car keys. There would be a trail through the house of things she had left behind her. And yet her whole goal in life was to be a wife and a mother.

I would think, *You want to be a wife and a mother, and you have to dig your way out every morning before you can leave the house?*

I would get mad and rant and rave and scream and yell at her. And none of it seemed to do the least bit of good. It didn't change her at all.

Today she is a grown woman with children of her own, and she and I are the best of friends. We do things together all the time. And she keeps a nice house. She actually succeeded in her goals. Imagine that! God brought her through.

Then there is Sandra, the daughter who now helps me in the ministry. When she was little, I thought she would drive me crazy because she was such a perfectionist. For example, she would sit in her room doing a homework paper. If she made one mistake, she would wad up her paper, throw it away, and start all over. If she had one pimple on her face, she would make a huge deal out of it. She would pick at it and put so much makeup on it that all she did was call attention to what she was trying to hide. With her, every hair had to be in place, which really irritated me.

One daughter bothered me because she wouldn't do anything, and the other one bothered me because she did everything.

Then there is our younger son, the one we call the baby, but who is a grown man now. I was so excited when that child finished high school. I felt like I had been let out of prison. I did *not* encourage him to go to college because he hated school and did poorly in it—so poorly that Dave and I had to hire private tutors for him.

I remember thinking, *What is this kid going to do in life to support himself?* But God had a plan all along.

We found out that our son is a hands-on learner. After graduation from high school, he came to work for us, and within a very short period of time he became the division manager of all our media. I keep commenting to Dave, "Can you believe he is doing this?"

I am sharing these stories with you to help you realize that where your kids are right now is not where they are going to end up. Your worrying about them only helps the problem; it doesn't help the answer.

Were you a mess when you were a teenager? Yet today you are reading this book, seeking God with all your heart. So there is hope for your kids.

Stop worrying. Stop complicating your life by trying to figure out everything. Just admit that you don't know, that you are not able, that you need God. Then go on living, and enjoy life while God is giving you the answers.

Pray and trust God, and He will show you what to do at the right time. He will show you because He is not a God who fails His children.[11] He is a God of faithfulness,[12] and He always comes through.

The way to win over the Joy Stealer of excessive reasoning is to be confident in God's ability to take care of everything that concerns you. The next Joy Keeper will help you grow in that confidence.

NINE

Joy Keeper #4: Be Confident in God

～

You will keep your joy if you remain confident in who you are in Christ. Then your confidence will be in Him, not in your own ability to understand everything that is happening.

The apostle Paul told us not to put our hope in our own ability but in Christ. He wrote, "For we [Christians] are the true circumcision, who worship God in spirit and by the Spirit of God and exult and glory and pride ourselves in Jesus Christ, and put no confidence or dependence [on what we are] in the flesh and on outward privileges and physical advantages and external appearances" (Philippians 3:3).

It takes a long time to get to the point where we have all our confidence in Christ and none in ourselves. But I can *finally* say that my joy is not from feeling better about myself, nor because of whom I know, what I wear, or what my natural gifts are. I am joyful because I have learned to look to Christ and know that whatever He asks me to do, whatever He leads me to do, I *can* do because He will give me strength.

Do you know, wherever you are in life, God gives you the grace to be there? If He has asked you to be there, He will give you the grace to be there. So Paul is really saying: "We put our confidence in Christ. We don't put our confidence in our own abilities." When we put our confidence in ourselves, we become foolish because our flesh is weak, but we are to be totally dependent on God's ability to guide us in the way we should go.

Paul wrote:

And that I may [actually] be found and known as *in Him*, not having any [self-achieved] righteousness that can be called my own, based on my obedience to the Law's demands (ritualistic uprightness and supposed right standing with God thus acquired), but possessing that [genuine righteousness] which comes through faith in Christ (the Anointed One), the [truly] right standing with God, which comes from God by [saving] faith. (Philippians 3:9, italics mine)

This statement, "in Christ" or "in Him," is repeated throughout the New Testament. It means to put all our faith, all our confidence, all our dependence on Him.

The Word also says, "Lean on, trust in, and be confident in the Lord with all your heart and mind and do not rely on your own insight or understanding. In all your ways know, recognize, and acknowledge Him, and He will direct and make straight and plain your paths" (Proverbs 3:5–6). When we look unto Him, we look away from ourselves for whatever it is we need to accomplish, for whatever we need to go through.

We look to Christ for our joy.

We look to Him for our peace.

Our hope is in Him.

There is no need for excessive reasoning or trying to figure out how or when our problems will be solved because everything we need is in Him.

OUR CONFIDENCE IS IN CHRIST

We all like to perform well. We all like to have a good reputation for behaving ourselves. But our confidence is not in our own righteousness.

The Bible talks about two kinds of righteousness. There is a righteousness one gets by following the law or by good works, which is the confidence we naturally try to obtain, but there is another righteousness that is available to us by grace, not by works. It is righteousness through Christ.

Paul said that he wanted to be found and known as *in Christ*, not having any brand of his own righteousness, but only the righteousness that Christ alone gives and ascribes. He understood that God would take care of all that concerned him because he was in right standing with God through Christ in him.

In other words, we don't have to feel that God is mad at us all the time because of our weaknesses and our faults. We can come before the throne of God and pray *boldly*, because we are in right standing with Him through our relationship with Jesus. We can have our needs met *while* we are in the process of growing spiritually.

Even though we don't understand everything that is happening around us, we can still pray with confidence. Even when we do something dumb, we can repent and still ask God to help us. We can pray:

> *Lord, I know this mess I'm in is my fault. I have nobody to blame but me, God, but I believe I am Your child and my righteousness is not in my own good record of perfection, but my righteousness with You is in Christ. I'm coming boldly to the throne, and I'm asking in Jesus' name for You to help get me out of this situation. Amen.*

I suffered a long time trying to earn the right to pray boldly, until I learned that we are not to put our confidence in our own flesh.

Paul even pointed out that we must avoid excessive reasoning about our own righteousness. He said that if anyone had a right to boast about following the law in order to be in right standing with God, he had more reason to boast than anyone.[1]

Paul did everything he knew to do to follow God's law, and he was so zealous that he persecuted those who didn't obey the standards of righteousness. But Paul later said, "Though I formerly blasphemed and persecuted and was shamefully and outrageously and aggressively insulting [to Him], nevertheless, I obtained mercy because I had acted out of ignorance in unbelief" (1 Timothy 1:13).

Paul's faith to pray boldly came through understanding that his confidence was in Christ alone. He understood

Isaiah's words that "all our righteousness (our best deeds of rightness and justice) is like filthy rags . . . and our iniquities, like the wind, take us away [far from God's favor, hurrying us toward destruction]" (Isaiah 64:6).

Once he understood who he was in Christ, Paul said:

> I count everything as loss compared to the possession of the priceless privilege (the overwhelming preciousness, the surpassing worth, and supreme advantage) of knowing Christ Jesus my Lord and of progressively becoming more deeply and intimately acquainted with Him [of perceiving and recognizing and understanding Him more fully and clearly]. For His sake I have lost everything and consider it all to be mere rubbish (refuse, dregs), in order that I may win (gain) Christ (the Anointed One), and that I may [actually] be found and known as in Him, *not having any [self-achieved] righteousness that can be called my own, based on my obedience to the Law's demands* (ritualistic uprightness and supposed right standing with God thus acquired), but *possessing that [genuine righteousness] which comes through faith in Christ.* (Philippians 3:8–9, italics mine)

Paul was saying, "Okay, all this stuff I had—all this record of good works, all the years of following the law—is useless. I count everything as loss compared to the priceless privilege of knowing Christ Jesus and becoming more deeply and intimately acquainted with Him."

If we want to have this righteousness, which only Christ can ascribe to us, then we have to forget about all the reasons we might deserve favors from God because of our own behavior. We still must strive to do things right, but not to get God to love us because He already loves us. But our prayers are answered because of Christ's righteousness, not because of self-righteousness before God.

I am not going from city to city to preach the gospel in order to gain points with God. I can continue holding conferences until the day Jesus comes back; I can work, work, work, and be on television all over the world, but I am no better in God's eyes than anybody else. Serving in the way I do doesn't earn me something that everyone else in the church doesn't earn as long as they follow God's will for their own lives.

I'm doing the work I do because I'm gifted to do it; I have the grace to do it, and all God is requiring of me is that I do what He has given me the grace to do. And all He is requiring of you is that you do what He gives you the grace to do.

I strive to live my personal life in the way I tell everybody else to live his or her life. I don't want to talk the talk and not walk the walk. But I know that my righteousness is not in the fact that I do my best to live right or because I'm a preacher. My righteousness is in Christ only, and no amount of good works or good behavior makes me right with God.

The law is perfect and holy. To *earn* righteousness so that we can pray boldly, we would have to keep every single solitary bit of God's law, and never make a mistake. Because if we break one law, then we are guilty of breaking all of it.[2]

We can never earn right standing with God by obedience to the law. We try to do things good because we love God, but we don't try to do good things to get God to love us. He loved us even before we were saved. The law is in place to help us live good lives; we are to use the law to discipline ourselves, but we cannot gain favor with God by trying to obey it. Our favor with God is based on our dependence on and confidence in Christ alone.

THE ANSWER IS FOUND IN CHRIST

Paul explained the wonderful assurance we have when our faith is in Christ. He wrote, "Yet now has [Christ, the Messiah] reconciled [you to God] in the body of His flesh through death, in order to *present you holy and faultless and irreproachable in His [the Father's] presence*." (Colossians 1:22, italics mine). Our joy is found in Christ, and that is the confidence God wants us to have every day.

We have to be careful not to secretly believe that God's favor is based on our good behavior. When we take on a self-righteous attitude, we begin to think we deserve something from God. Then when trials or difficulties come into our lives, we think, *Well, how could God let this happen after all these years that I've served Him?*

Can you see how this would keep us from joy? If, deep inside, we secretly believe we deserve something from God that we are not getting, we will become resentful and then we won't be bold in standing before Him. Instead, we will fall into excessive reasoning, trying to figure out why we lost our blessings.

Blessings are stolen, not lost; the Word clearly says that the devil is a thief who comes to steal from us. We keep our joy in spite of any loss because we are confident in God's promise to care for us. We can remain joyful because we know we do not *lose* God's provision because of imperfection. We are righteous in Christ, and He remains constantly in right standing with God on our behalf. Hebrews 4:14–15 explains:

> Inasmuch then as we have a great High Priest Who has [already] ascended and passed through the heavens, Jesus the Son of God, let us hold fast *our confession [of faith in Him].* For we do not have a High Priest Who is unable to understand and sympathize and have a shared feeling with our weaknesses and infirmities and liability to the assaults of temptation, but One Who has been tempted in every respect as we are, yet without sinning. (Italics mine)

Since our faith is in our High Priest, Jesus, and not in the false hope that we *deserve* something from God, we are to pursue God's blessings through bold prayer. Hebrews 4:16–5:1 instructs:

> Let us then fearlessly and confidently and boldly draw near to the throne of grace (the throne of God's unmerited favor to us sinners), that *we may receive mercy [for our failures]* and *find grace to help in good time for every need* [appropriate help and well-timed help, *coming just when we need it].* For every high priest chosen from among men is appointed to act on behalf of men in things relating to God, to offer both gifts and sacrifices for sins. (Italics mine)

Paul was trying to tell people that he'd had all the advantages a person could have. He had every reason to depend on himself, but he knew works of the flesh did not give him favor with God. Self-righteousness is not what we need; we cannot earn the grace of God's favor. Right standing with God comes through faith in Jesus Christ.

Paul's hope should be our own:

[For my determined purpose is] that I may know Him [that I may progressively become more deeply and intimately acquainted with Him, perceiving and recognizing and understanding the wonders of His Person more strongly and more clearly], and *that I may in that same way come to know the power outflowing from His resurrection* [which it exerts over believers], and that I may so share His sufferings *as to be continually transformed [in spirit into His likeness* even] to His death, [in the hope] that if possible I may attain to the [spiritual and moral] resurrection [that lifts me] out from among the dead *[even while in the body]*. Not that I have now attained [this ideal], or have already been made perfect, but I press on to lay hold of (grasp) and make my own, that for which Christ Jesus (the Messiah) has laid hold of me and made me His own. (Philippians 3:10–12, italics mine)

REST IN GOD

Instead of having great confidence in ourselves, we need to learn to rest in God. Our daily prayer should be, "God, I need You in everything I do. Apart from You, I can do nothing."

I always depend on God to make clear to me what message to share in my meetings, but sometimes it seems I am not hearing Him. Instead of getting worried or anxious, I've learned to just relax and trust Him. In faith, I just admit He is not showing me what to do, and I know I'm not going to get answers by works of the flesh. So I stop thinking about it for a while and wait on God to show me in His timing. It takes faith to give up trying to plan every detail. I have learned to let it alone and do something else while I'm waiting on God.

Often when I am resting, all of a sudden I hear God's answer to my question. In ten minutes I have a complete outline of all that God wants me to cover. Life is easy and full of joy when we depend on God! I could stay up half the night trying to work out a perfect plan, but it wouldn't have any power if God wasn't in it. When God shows us the way, it is easy.

God holds the entire universe together. Everything in the world is supported and upheld by the power of His Word. If He can keep all that together, surely He can keep our lives together. Psalm 103:12–14 says:

> As far as the east is from the west, so far has He removed our transgressions from us. As a father loves and pities his children, so the Lord loves and pities those who fear Him [with reverence, worship, and awe]. For He knows our frame, He [earnestly] remembers and imprints [on His heart] that we are dust.

God removes all that makes us unrighteous (our transgressions) and sends it as far away as the east is from the west. How far is the east from the west? A long way!

God knows our weaknesses, and He remembers that we

are but dust. We put a lot more pressure on ourselves than God would ever put on us.

When my son was small, he decided to do something nice for me. He got a bowl of water and went out on the porch. Soon he came to me and said, "Mommy, I washed the windows for you." The porch was wet. He was wet. The windows were smeared up. But he did it because he loved me.

God reminded me of this one time. He said, "Do you remember what you did afterward? You sent your son off to get cleaned up and then you went and cleaned up his mess when he wasn't looking." God showed me that He does the same with us.

God is aware of our imperfections, and He receives what we do out of love for Him. He will cover our tracks, clean up our messes, and hide them so we won't even realize what a mess we made. He does this because we are in Christ, Christ is in Him, and He is in us.

Jesus explained it this way:

I will not leave you as orphans [comfortless, desolate, bereaved, forlorn, helpless]; I will come [back] to you. Just a little while now, and the world will not see Me any more, but you will see Me; because I live, you will live also. At that time [when that day comes] you will know [for yourselves] that *I am in My Father, and you [are] in Me, and I [am] in you.*" (John 14:18-20, italics mine)

If God asks, "Why should I let you into heaven?" the only right answer is, "Because I'm in Christ." If God asks, "Why should I answer your prayers?" the right answer is,

"Because I'm in Christ." If God asks, "Why should I help you?" the only right answer is, "Because I'm in Christ."

Jesus wants us to come *fearlessly, confidently, and boldly* to the Father for mercy for our failures and grace for every need we have. He understands our weaknesses and faults. He understands that we are not going to manifest perfection every day. But we can ask God to forgive us for the mistakes we make and then go boldly before the throne to ask God to meet our needs.

ASK THAT YOUR JOY WILL BE COMPLETE

Jesus said, "Up to this time you have not asked a [single] thing in My Name [as presenting all that I AM]; but now ask and keep on asking and you will receive, *so that your joy (gladness, delight) may be full and complete*" (John 16:24, italics mine).

I believe there are people who are not receiving from God what He wants them to have because they won't ask boldly of Him. They make weak, faithless requests. I've had people come forward for prayer and say: "Is it okay if I ask for two things?" Their uncertainty is sad to me because Jesus clearly told us to ask so that our joy would be complete.

To pray boldly is to say: "God, I am going to be right here before Your throne. I am going ask for everything You know I need, and everything You want to give to me. Not because of greed, but because I am learning to be bold as You said we should be."

I want whatever God wants to give me spiritually, emotionally, financially, physically, and mentally. I certainly don't pray that because I think *I'm* worthy. I know what I am, and I know what I'm not, but I also know who He is, and I know my confidence is not in myself; it's in Him.

My joy is not from having things that God gives to me, but from loving God intimately and knowing that He wants me to be totally dependent on Him for everything I need. I know I get up every day and do the best I can, and I am not going to be robbed. I am going to receive what Jesus died to give me.

For example, a few years ago, I stepped out in faith and prayed a bold prayer that even sounded crazy to me. I said, "God, I'm asking You to let me help every single person on the face of the earth."

My mind said: *Now that is stupid.* But I kept praying that prayer anyway, and our television ministry has expanded greatly since that time. It has been a mega-expansion; one station that we added after that increased our coverage to six hundred million people in India alone.

I don't know *how* God is going to let me help every person on the face of the earth, but I would rather ask for a lot and get part of it than ask for a little and get all of it. The Bible says that we do not have because we do not ask.[3]

Practice this Joy Keeper of being confident in God as you face new trials. The next time you are tempted to be anxious, remember that excessive reasoning will rob you of joy.

Don't let trials tempt you to worry excessively as you try to reason your way out of them. James said, "Consider it wholly joyful, my brethren, whenever you are enveloped in *or* encounter trials of any sort or fall into various temptations" (James 1:2). He explained that trials prove our faith and bring out endurance, steadfastness, and patience.

He also said to let trials do a thorough work in us and to ask God for wisdom. James said that God will give wisdom to you without reproaching you or finding fault with you.

Be bold (and confident in God) when you pray; don't be double-minded when you ask for His blessings. Don't think, *I wonder if I have been righteous enough for God to grant my request?* Just ask for what you need, boldly and in faith, without wavering, hesitating, or doubting, knowing that your righteousness is in Christ.

In chapter 1 verse 12, James writes: "Blessed (happy, to be envied) is the man who is patient under trial and stands up under temptation, for when he has stood the test and been approved, he will receive [the victor's] crown of life which God has promised to those who love Him." In other words, trials do not require excessive reasoning that steals our joy. We can be confident that trials do not come just because we are unrighteous. Trials produce opportunities for us to receive the victor's crown, so count them all joy.

In the next chapter, I will be sharing with you things I have learned about the Joy Stealer of anger and how to control it. I pray that you can recognize if you have a problem with anger and if you do, learn the next Joy Keeper and trust God to help you overcome it.

TEN

Joy Stealer #5:
Ungodly Anger

~

Anger is an emotion often characterized by feelings of great displeasure, indignation, hostility, wrath, and vengeance. Many times anger is how we express our dissatisfaction with life. It is the fruit of rotten roots, and it steals our joy.

Some roots that lead to anger include insecurity, fear of confrontation, and a feeling of being controlled by a job or other people and their problems. One of the primary roots of anger often stems from the family. Angry people come from angry families because they learn from their role models and perpetuate the same behavior in their own lives, eventually passing it on to their children.

If you have anger in your heart or your home, don't feel condemned. We are never going to run out of things to be angry about. In fact, God has equipped us with the feeling and emotion of anger for a reason.

When kept in balance, the emotion of anger serves a

good purpose. If we weren't able to become angry, we would never know when someone was mistreating us. That is the purpose of anger. Like pain, it is there to warn us that something is not right.

Our job is not so much to try to get rid of anger, but to learn how to handle it. The Word teaches us the proper way to deal with this emotion: "When angry, do not sin; do not ever let your wrath (your exasperation, your fury or indignation) last until the sun goes down" (Ephesians 4:26).

My family is very close, and we enjoy our friendship and being together. But it wasn't always that way. At one time our household was filled with anger and strife, bitterness, and unforgiveness. Thankfully, we learned long ago how to handle and deal with these negative emotions, and the result has been tremendous blessings from God.

If you want the great and mighty things God has for you, you must get to the root of your anger and deal with it. God wants to bless you, but anger opens the door for the devil to try to stop those blessings and keep you from accomplishing the will of God in your life.[1]

BE GLAD, NOT MAD

Have you ever thought about how hard it is to be angry and joyful at the same time? Either you are going to be glad, or you are going to be mad.

Anger is passion that people often feel uncomfortable discussing. Actually, it is one of our strongest passions, beginning with a feeling and then manifesting into words and actions. Anger is an emotion that we all experience, and sometimes we get angry quickly and easily. But feeling anger is not the sin—it is what we do with the anger that is important.

God doesn't tell us not to get angry, but He does tell us what to do about our anger.

Ephesians 4:26 gives us a good idea of how important it is not to *stay* angry: "When angry, do not sin." What does that mean? One thing it means is that when you experience the emotion of anger, you shouldn't act on your feelings. Don't be led and motivated by them. Don't say what you would like to say or do what you would like to do because that is what causes your problem.

You may be thinking, *But I can't help it; I'm angry.*

It's important to understand something about emotions: What goes up comes down. Emotions are fickle, and what bothers you today might seem quite different tomorrow. Wait for emotions to subside and then decide what you should do.

Dave has a philosophy that he used to share with me when I got angry. I used to think it was crazy; now I understand. He would say to me, "Why do you want to stay mad at me? This time next week, you'll be talking to me again just as though nothing happened. So why don't you go ahead and do it now?"

That was true.

His philosophy is: "If you are going to be friendly with me next week, why waste two or three days staying angry at me now? Let's just go ahead and be friendly now."

Why couldn't I do that? Because I *felt* anger, and I *acted* on my feelings. But after a few days those feelings changed.

GOD IS OUR VINDICATOR

People rightfully become angry at injustice, but we must learn that God is our Vindicator.[2] Trying to vindicate ourselves only causes pain on top of pain.

I can testify that this is true. I was sexually abused for many years and endured many other injustices as well. I was angry, bitter, and resentful. I had a chip on my shoulder and could not maintain good relationships. Trying to vindicate myself only continued to ruin my life, but when I finally turned my case over to God entirely, He brought an outstanding reward into my life for the pain of my past. This Word proved true for me: "Instead of your [former] shame you shall have a twofold recompense; instead of dishonor and reproach [your people] shall rejoice in their portion. Therefore in their land they shall possess double [what they had forfeited]; everlasting joy shall be theirs" (Isaiah 61:7).

If you and I will learn to get angry without sinning, then we will actually allow whatever is causing us to be angry to build godly character inside us.

I am quite sure there are a few things that anger God, yet He doesn't act out His anger. That's why He tells us, "When angry, do not sin; do not ever let your wrath (your exasperation, your fury or indignation) last until the sun goes down" (Ephesians 4:26).

Now I don't know about you, but I'm glad this verse is in the Bible because it helps us to build character by giving us a guideline to follow in handling our anger: Let go of anger before bedtime. There is only one problem: What happens when we become good and mad just before bedtime? If we become mad in the morning, at least we have all day to get over it. But when we become mad close to bedtime, we have to make a quick decision.

Why is it so bad for us to go to bed angry? I think it is because while we sleep, what we are angry about has time to get a hold on us and take root in us. But the Word says, "Leave no [such] room or foothold for the devil [give no opportunity to him]" (Ephesians 4:27). This verse tells us what happens if we refuse to get over our anger by bedtime: It opens a door for the devil; it gives Satan a foothold. Once Satan gets a foothold in our lives, then he can move on to a stronghold.

All anger, regardless of its cause, has the same effect on our lives. It upsets us, causing us to feel pressure. That is one way Satan dupes us into losing our joy. Keeping anger locked inside and pretending it doesn't exist can even be dangerous to our health. It usually doesn't bother the person who makes us angry; it just hurts us.

You may wonder, *Well, if I am mad, what should I do about it?*

Get over it!

Think about all the people you have made angry. Think about something to be glad about. Let your gladness overcome your madness. Let your joy overcome your sadness.

You may think, *That's easy for you to say, but you're not in my situation.*

I may not be in your situation, but you are not in my situation either. We all have different situations. If you are

116

going to live a joyful, victorious life, you have to do so by choice and not by feeling.

In Deuteronomy 30:19 the Lord tells us, "I have set before you life and death, the blessings and the curses; therefore choose life." Choose life by refusing to give in to anger. Take responsibility for your anger and learn to deal with it—process it and bring closure to it, and that will relieve the pressure.

TALK TO YOURSELF

One way you can get over being angry is by talking to yourself. You can talk yourself into anger, and you can talk yourself out of it.

For example, a woman's husband may do something to hurt her feelings, so she sits around and talks to herself about it: "I'm just sick and tired of him treating me this way. I don't think it's right. I do everything for him, and he doesn't do anything for me. He never helps me around the house. He never remembers my birthday or our wedding anniversary. He never thinks of anyone but himself. That's it. I've had it with him. If he thinks I'm going to go on putting up with him, he's got another *think* coming!"

Before she knows it, she is spitfire mad. And it may be over some little thing that doesn't amount to much.

Have you ever talked yourself into being angry when somebody mistreated you or was rude to you or did something to you that you didn't like? You can talk yourself out of being angry when that happens. Just get away from the thing that is making you mad for a few minutes and start talking to yourself in a different way.

You could tell yourself, "Okay, self, just settle down. This is just the devil trying to get you upset. Don't give him an open door. There's too much at stake here. Don't go getting mad, losing your temper, and saying a lot of things you are going to be sorry for later. Consider the source."

Remember that Satan is the source of your anger—he is the enemy, not some person.[3]

Ephesians 5:15–17 teaches us to live purposefully, and to make the most of each opportunity to grasp what is the will of the Lord for us. The Word says, "Be filled with the Spirit; speaking to yourselves in psalms and hymns and spiritual songs" (Ephesians 5:18–19 KJV). I believe we all need to preach little sermons to ourselves at times.

I have to back off when I feel myself getting into something that is making me upset, especially when it doesn't involve me. I say to myself, "You know what, Joyce? This is really none of your business. So why don't you just leave it alone? What those people do is none of your business."

Learn to talk to yourself in that way. Learn to tell yourself, "It's none of my business."

Are You Listening?

We are all supposed to listen more than we talk. Otherwise, we would have been created with two mouths and one ear. Think how funny we would look if we had two mouths and one ear.

There is a lesson in the following passage: "Understand [this], my beloved brethren. Let every man be quick to hear [a ready listener], slow to speak, slow to take offense and to get angry. For man's anger does not promote the righteousness God [wishes and requires]" (James 1:19–20). In these verses God is saying to us, "Listen more than you talk. And be slow to become offended and slow to get angry because offense and anger do not promote My righteousness."[4]

If you have a quick, bad temper, you can do something about it. Read everything you can get your hands on about anger.[5] If necessary, fast and pray until you get over that anger. If you cannot control your own spirit, you are never going to be able to enjoy your life.

TAKE CONTROL OF YOUR ANGER

"He who is slow to anger is better than the mighty, he who rules his [own] spirit than he who takes a city" (Proverbs 16:32). This verse illustrates the power of controlling our anger. To do that, we need to be able to control our mouths. We need to be able to control our thoughts. We need to be able to control our passions, our emotions, and our tempers. God has given us self-control.

Many people don't even know that is an option. When I first started studying the Bible, I didn't know it was an option either. I thought the way I felt dictated my actions. When I got mad, I would just wait until the feeling decided to go away instead of refusing to allow it to steal my joy and control me. Sometimes it would be a few days before my anger subsided, and sometimes it would be a few weeks.

Now I know I can decide to get over my anger. I can talk to myself, and I can pray and ask God to help me, to give me grace and strength.[6]

We don't need to let anger shut down the power of God in our lives.

As believers, we have been equipped with God's power to walk in the fruit of the Spirit,[7] love the unlovely, forgive those who have hurt us, and remain stable in spite of our circumstances. With His help, we can make a choice to do what is right. When we do what is right, lots of right things will happen in our lives. Right action brings right fruit. Wrong action brings wrong fruit. Our anger does not promote the righteousness that God desires, but controlling our anger does.

BE LIKE GOD

Do you think God is sitting in the heavens today angry and crying and depressed? No, that is not God's nature. God is joyful. He is strong because He is joyful. And the Bible teaches us that the joy of the Lord is our strength.[8]

Another principle we are taught in the Bible is that we are to be imitators of God.[9] So however God is, that is the way we should be. *Clarke's Commentary* describes God as "holy, just, wise, good, and perfect" and adds "so must the soul be that sprang from him."[10]

We can get a good idea of God's attributes by looking closely at the following Scripture verses:

The Lord is merciful and gracious, slow to anger and plenteous in mercy and loving-kindness. He will not always chide or be contending, neither will He keep His anger forever or hold a grudge. He has not dealt with us after our sins nor rewarded us according to our iniquities. For as the heavens are high above the earth, so great are His mercy and loving-kindness toward those who reverently and worshipfully fear Him. As far as the east is from the west, so far has He removed our transgressions from us. (Psalm 103:8–12)

Look at verse 8 again: "The Lord is merciful and gracious, slow to anger and plenteous in mercy and loving-kindness."

If you become angry at someone over an injustice, one way to get over it is to imitate God and choose to give that person mercy. Just think, *I am going to give you something you don't deserve. I am going to let go of what you did to me. I am going to bless you and in the process bless myself.*

Showing mercy to others is wise because we often need mercy ourselves. Remember, if we sow mercy we will reap mercy.[11]

Some time ago I was thinking about the worldly phrase "To err is human, to forgive divine."[12] That is so true. When we can let go of an offense, it is a godly thing. Forgiveness is an ability that God has, and God gives us that ability if we will but operate in it.

Psalm 103:9 continues, "He will not always chide or be contending, neither will He keep His anger forever or hold a grudge." We see from this verse that even God has righteous anger—anger against sin, injustice, rebellion, and

121

pettiness. Aren't you glad that even if we do make Him mad, He doesn't stay mad, and He doesn't hold a grudge? God wants us to be the same way. What we receive from Him, He expects us to give to others. God never expects us to give away anything He has not first given us. But what He gives us, He does expect us to give away.

God gives you forgiveness, and He expects you to give it away. He gives you mercy, and He expects you to give it away. He doesn't stay angry with you, and He expects you not to stay angry with other people. He is slow to become angry, and He expects you to be slow to become angry.

You and I can be like God because His character is in us.[13] We must believe that—because otherwise, the devil will inject his thoughts into our minds: *You can't be like God. You can't be merciful and gracious, slow to anger, plenteous in mercy and loving-kindness. You can't be forgiving.*

That is why we must read our Bibles and fill ourselves with the Word on a regular basis. I know from personal experience that the Word of God changes people because it has changed me completely, and it will do the same for you. But it must be learned and applied in our daily lives. Otherwise, we will listen to the devil, believe his lies, and think, *It's true. I can't be like that; nobody can be like that but God. I can't help it if I'm angry. I can't help it if I'm contentious, if I stay angry and hold a grudge. I can't help it if I feel anger and resentment toward others.*

Yes, you can. That type of thinking is an excuse that keeps us in bondage. Those wrong thought patterns can prevent us from finishing our course with joy.[14] The truth is that anger will poison our joy level if left unchallenged. Anger is a negative emotion that breathes death everywhere it is permitted to remain. But we can receive help from God through His Son, Jesus, and His Word, and be totally set free.

BE DELIVERED FROM ANGER

Consider the following verses: "Cease from anger and forsake wrath; fret not yourself—it tends only to evildoing. For evildoers shall be cut off, but those who wait and hope and look for the Lord [in the end] shall inherit the earth" (Psalm 37:8–9).

If you think you might have a bad temper or you get mad quickly and easily, no matter what has caused your anger, I encourage you to face it, take responsibility for it, and deal with it properly, beginning with prayer.

In fact, I feel that the Lord wants me to pause and say a prayer for you to help you stop anger from destroying the wonderful plan He has for your life. Let's pray right now:

Father, I pray for the person reading this book who has a bad temper or a quick temper, who gets offended easily or angry often.

When they do get angry, they don't know how to let go of it quickly. I pray, Lord, that You will do a mighty work inside them. I pray that they will hear Your voice speaking in their hearts and saying, "Learn in this area. Gain victory in this area."

Father, I know that You have many great and wonderful things You want to do in their life and through them and for them. But this is an area that needs to be resolved and settled.

I thank You, Lord, for breaking this bondage of anger that is out of control and for giving them Your grace and mercy. In Jesus' name I pray. Amen.

Once the Joy Stealer of anger has been confronted in your life, fill your heart with forgiveness toward those who offend you. The next chapter will encourage you with what God has to say about the Joy Keeper of forgiveness.

ELEVEN

Joy Keeper #5: Be Quick to Forgive

⤜⤏

Joy is restored to your life when you learn how to forgive and forget, and the two virtues go together. God tells us that He forgives our sins and puts them as far as the east is from the west,[1] *and He remembers them no more.*[2]

Frequently, we try to forgive people, but forgiveness can't do its redemptive work because we want to remember what they did to us. We continue to think and talk about them. Remembering a past offense reopens the wound and feeds anger; anger in turn feeds unforgiveness.

A lady once shared with me how God taught her a valuable lesson through forgiving her son. Her son had disappointed her and hurt her in many different ways. And, being a godly woman, she got to the point where she knew that she had to forgive him, and the day came when she finally felt able to do that.

She was so proud of herself for forgiving him that she wrote him a long letter—to tell him of *all the things* for which she was forgiving him. She also told everybody else *all the things* for which she was forgiving him. And she kept thinking to herself about *all the things* she had been able to let go of concerning him.

One day, while she was thinking about her son and *all these things* she had forgiven, and how good she was because she had forgiven him, the Lord prompted her to read 1 Corinthians.

As she was reading chapter 13, what we know as the "Love Chapter," she came to verse 5, which says that love "takes no account of the evil done to it [it pays no attention to a suffered wrong]."

Then the Lord told her, "You're one of the best accountants I know."

I'm sure most of us are guilty of keeping good records of offenses we have suffered. But if we want joy to operate in our lives, we will have to learn how to forgive *and* forget. Forgiveness needs to be a lifestyle. Why do we need to forgive other people? Because our faith won't work if we don't. We end up torturing ourselves if we don't forgive others. We make ourselves miserable when we hold grudges.

We also need to forgive others just to be in obedience to God. If we don't, unforgiveness blocks our fellowship with Him, and that prevents our own spiritual growth. Besides (if that is not enough), unforgiveness is spiritual filthiness; it is like dirt and mud on our spirit.

First of all, we certainly need to forgive other people who have hurt us. It is important that we don't let bitterness, resentment, and unforgiveness become stored up in us. We even need to forgive people who hurt us a long, long time ago, and we need to forgive people who are hurting us on a daily basis.

In fact, if you have lost joy because of unforgiveness, I suggest that you start forgiving people right away. Make a list of people you need to forgive. Ask the Lord to give you the power to forgive these people, and then let it go.

FORGIVE YOURSELF

Second, you may need to forgive yourself. As a young Christian, I would cry out to God to forgive me for the same thing every night. And one night, the Lord spoke to me: "Joyce, I forgave you the first time you asked Me. You need to forgive yourself."

Think about that. God forgives us the first time we ask Him. But, we need to *receive* the forgiveness that God is trying to give us.

I know some people who read this book were abused in the past. Some who read this book may even have abused others at some point. Abused people often turn around and abuse others. You may be on one or both sides of that kind of pain. If you are holding on to any *unforgiveness* against yourself or others, you will miss the joy God wants you to have. Let it go!

Many women who come to my meetings, or who listen to my messages on radio or television, admit they have had abortions. Many have been in prostitution in the past. Some people have been involved in sexual perversion or adultery. Some had premarital relations with the persons they are married to now, some became pregnant before marriage, and now their marriages are affected because they still have not forgiven themselves or their spouses.

If any of these circumstances, or similar situations, apply to you, I wouldn't be surprised if you have already asked God to forgive you hundreds and hundreds of times. Yet you still lack joy because you won't forgive yourself. I challenge you to forgive yourself and receive that forgiveness you have been crying out to God to give you all this time. Take it. You're asking God to give you something He wants you to have. Now, take it.

Many individuals resist forgiveness and say, "I don't deserve it." Of course we don't deserve *anything* God gives us! We might as well just establish that *we have absolutely no way of deserving God's blessings.* But grace is free:

> For it is by free grace (God's unmerited favor) that you are saved (delivered from judgment and made partakers of Christ's salvation) through [your] faith. And this [salvation] is not of yourselves [of your own doing, it came not through your own striving], but it is the gift of God. (Ephesians 2:8)

Many people will not forgive themselves because they feel they have disappointed God. My own husband felt that way many years ago. He has a strong, powerful relationship with God, but there was a time when he didn't take it quite as seriously as he should have. During that time, he had a devastating experience that caused him to think the presence of God had lifted from his life. Then he went through a season of guilt and condemnation because he felt he was being punished for disappointing God. It was a difficult struggle for him.

Finally, he was in a Bible class where the pastor was teaching on guilt and condemnation. Knowing that God did not condemn him, Dave forgave himself and was set free from the guilt he felt. Once healed and restored, Dave started going forward into all that God had for him.

GO FORWARD WITH GOD

You can't go forward with God if you are going to hold against yourself the things you've done in the past. *The only way you can go forward is by letting go of what is behind you.*

We cannot buy our freedom from guilt. We cannot buy forgiveness with works of righteousness, yet we try to do that. If we misbehave, we feel as if we can't even pray until we do a few things to get back in God's good graces.

But feelings of guilt do not buy forgiveness.

Guilt is a carnal, fleshly way of trying to pay for forgiveness. People think if they *feel bad enough* about something they did, they will *earn* forgiveness. Some people try so hard to pay for their sins through guilt that they even *refuse* to enjoy life.

I was like that for a long time. If everything wasn't perfect, I didn't allow myself to have any fun. I thought I had to earn joy. But I learned that I could not buy forgiveness by punishing myself with self-rejection.

Isaiah 55:1 is worth rejoicing over. It says: "Wait and listen, everyone who is thirsty! Come to the waters; and he who has no money, come, buy and eat! Yes, come, buy [priceless, spiritual] wine and milk without money and without price [simply for the self-surrender that accepts the blessing]."

You may be thirsty for forgiveness. God invites everyone who is thirsty to come to His waters. Everyone who is hungry can come and eat at His table. The preceding Scripture is about those who have no way to purchase what they need from God—and that would be every one of us.

What's the price to receive blessings from God? All we need is available to us simply for the self-surrender to accept the blessing. I love that.

Just make a decision that you are going to forgive yourself, and get on with God's program. To be released from the emotional prison of anger and unforgiveness, I encourage you to pray this prayer:

Okay, God, I surrender to You. I will quit trying to earn Your goodness. I will let You bless me and give to me what I don't deserve.

I receive Your forgiveness for my sins, my failures, my shortcomings, my faults, and my slipups. As You have forgiven me, I also forgive those who have hurt me, not because they deserve to be forgiven, but because Your grace is flowing in and out of my life.

I pray that You will bless those who have hurt me so they, too, will come to know the joy of Your forgiveness. Amen.

Isaiah 61:1 says that Jesus is anointed to preach the gospel of good tidings to the poor, to bind up and heal broken hearts, to proclaim liberty to physical and spiritual captives, and to open the prison and the eyes of those who are bound. This means that Jesus has opened the prison door of unforgiveness. Unforgiveness will no longer hold you in bondage. Jesus not only opens the door for you, but He also opens your eyes so that you can see your freedom.

Some prison doors have been open for years, but believers are still sitting captive in the cell because they don't see that it is open. They haven't understood their freedom in Christ. Make sure you are not one of those captives.

It is no accident that you are reading this book. Jesus is opening your eyes to see that you are free from whatever has kept you from being full of joy. The Word of God is your key to open any prison door that keeps you bound. Don't be addicted to being against yourself. Give it up. Don't be addicted to guilt and condemnation. Don't beat on yourself about something for which God has forgiven you.

Jesus told Paul that His purpose in calling Paul to preach the gospel was "to open their eyes that they may turn from darkness to light and from the power of Satan to God, so that they may thus *receive forgiveness and release from their sins* and a place and portion among those who are consecrated and purified by faith in Me" (Acts 26:18, italics mine).

Jesus came to open our eyes to bring us out of darkness into the light. The Bible doesn't say that we might *earn* forgiveness or *get* forgiveness, but that we might *receive* forgiveness.

This purpose is what Jesus was talking about on the cross when He said, "It is finished!" There is no more sacrifice that can be made for our joy. We cannot add our sacrifice to His. His was a perfect sacrifice. It's over, finished, done with—now, we need only to *receive* God's provision, as the following Scripture passages explain:

- But to as many as did *receive and welcome Him*, He gave the authority (power, privilege, right) to become the children of God, that is, to those who believe in (adhere to, trust in, and rely on) His name. (John 1:12, italics mine)
- For everything God has created is good, and nothing is to be thrown away or refused if it is received with thanksgiving. (1 Timothy 4:4)
- So get rid of all uncleanness and the rampant outgrowth of wickedness, and in a humble (gentle, modest) spirit receive and welcome the Word which implanted and rooted [in your hearts] contains the power to save your souls. (James 1:21)

We need to learn how to be good receivers.

FORGIVE GOD

The third Person you may need to forgive is God. That might sound as foreign to you as it did to me the first time I heard somebody say in a prayer line, "I have unforgiveness against God." But people can develop bitterness and resentment toward God, especially if they have had a lot of disappointments in their lives.

People blame God for their unhappiness, and the devil wants you to blame God if you aren't happy. He wants to create a rift between you and God so that you will lose your joy.

Sometimes people try to get things they want from God by imitating what they have seen others do. Then they get upset when He doesn't answer the way they think He should. But by copying others' actions, they're doing things God never told *them* to do. Don't be mad at God for not blessing something He didn't tell you to do. And don't blame Him for things the devil has brought into your life. If you have unforgiveness in your heart against God, give it up and let it go.

You will not be disappointed with God if you wait in faith to hear a personal word, a "rhema,"[3] from Him. Romans 10:17 teaches: "So faith comes by hearing [what is told], and what is heard comes by the preaching [of the message that came from the lips] of Christ (the Messiah Himself)."

If you want joy in your life, you have to believe that God is good and that He rewards those who diligently seek Him.[4]

Joy will fill you when you quit demanding answers to why bad things have happened to you. For years, I asked God to tell me *why* my childhood was filled with abuse. I wondered *why* God didn't intervene. *Why* didn't He do something to stop the abuse if He is so mighty and powerful?

I had a big chip on my shoulder, which gave me an attitude that everyone owed me something. But I couldn't have a decent relationship with anybody until the truth of God's Word set me free from needing answers to those questions. I began doing things God's way, and He Himself became my reward.

God wants to bless every person. God is blessing my life. He is doing some powerful and mighty things that I am enjoying. No matter what is going on in your life right now, no matter how badly it hurts, don't blame God. You may not always understand what is happening, but God is perfect. He is good, and He is right. Fault and error are either the cause of mankind or instigated by the devil.

If you have been upset with God, I encourage you to give it up to Him. This may seem odd, because we are always asking God to forgive us, but simply pray, *God, I forgive You. My problems are not Your fault. You are my answer.*

Of course, God does not need your forgiveness, but you may need to forgive.

In 1989, my faith in God's goodness was severely tested when I was diagnosed with cancer. I went in for a routine checkup, and I certainly wasn't expecting this report. Two weeks later, I was in the hospital having an operation.

The temptation to be bitter came to me. I wanted to reason with God, to tell Him I didn't deserve this. I wanted to remind Him that I work for Him. Didn't He remember me?

Sometimes we want to tell God all the good things we've done. But God told me what to say to Him during that time. He said, "All I want to hear you say is, 'I love You. I know You love me. I trust You. God is good. This is the day the Lord has made. I will rejoice and be glad in it.' "

Of course God brought me through the cancer. I've had victory, and everything is wonderful again. But if I had become bitter toward God, I fully believe I would not be in ministry as I am today.

The devil wants you to blame God for your problems, but don't you do it. Unforgiveness is like taking poison and hoping your enemy will die. Be free; forgive everyone who has ever hurt you—from a long time ago or even recently. Decide to forgive everyone, forgive yourself, and forgive

God. Then forget about it and embrace the joy of the Lord in your life.

FORGET AND BE JOYFUL

The word *forget* means "1: to lose the remembrance of: be unable to think of or recall; 2: to treat with inattention or disregard; and 3: to disregard intentionally: overlook."[5]

When God tells us we are to forget what lies behind us, I don't think He means we will be *unable* to remember; I believe He is encouraging us to intentionally *choose not to remember*.

Forgetting is a choice. The Bible says to choose to remember the better things in life: "For the rest, brethren, whatever is true, whatever is worthy of reverence and is honorable and seemly, whatever is just, whatever is pure, whatever is lovely and lovable, whatever is kind and winsome and gracious, if there is any virtue and excellence, if there is anything worthy of praise, think on and weigh and take account of these things [fix your minds on them]" (Philippians 4:8). In other words, God is saying, "These are the things that will give you joy."

To forget old wounds means to "fail to mention them." It means that we won't keep account of them. When Dave and I used to argue, I would bring up something that had hurt me from the first year of our marriage!

He would look at me and say, "How do you remember all that stuff?"

Remembering wasn't hard at all. I meditated on it while doing the dishes and laundry! I rehearsed it. I practiced it.

Just like the mother who was keeping account of her son's offenses, I kept careful accounting, too. When Dave and I got into the war zone, I didn't have to go digging around for my anger—it was fresh at hand. I had grooves worn into my brain from days spent dwelling on my anger.

If we want joy, we must have a "lack of concern" for old offenses. Paul taught:

> I do not consider, brethren, that I have captured and made it my own [yet]; but one thing I do [it is my one aspiration]: *forgetting what lies behind and straining forward to what lies ahead, I press on* toward the goal to win the [supreme and heavenly] prize to which God in Christ Jesus is calling us upward. (Philippians 3:13–14, italics mine)

You may *feel* as though you can't stop thinking about whatever makes you angry. But you can *choose* to stop thinking about it. The Bible says to cast down imaginations and every high and lofty thing that exalts itself against the knowledge of God.[6]

You can almost get addicted to pouting about all the things everybody has done to you. But you can also pray, and God will help you. He will give you the power to think about things that will bring benefits and blessings to you.

Thinking on old wounds from the past will not benefit you; bad memories do not help you live a joyful life. You need to purposely form the good habit of thinking on God's promises instead.

Decide to forgive. Realize that some people in your life will need to be forgiven again and again, some many times a day.

You will feel joy when you forgive the reckless offenses of others.

You will feel joy when you forgive the people whose personalities rub you the wrong way.

You will feel joy even if you are willing to forgive someone seven times for the same offense.[7]

There will always be people in your life who will give you opportunities to be offended. Even if no one is lying to you, or stealing from you, there are still crazy drivers, rude shoppers, and people who push ahead of you in line who give you new opportunities every day to feel the joy of forgiveness!

If you want to walk in joy, you will have to walk in forgiveness. The Holy Ghost will give you the power to enjoy your life.[8] If you really want joy to abound, then forgive your enemies outright. Jesus said:

> I say to you who are listening now to Me: [in order to heed, make it a practice to] love your enemies, treat well (do good to, act nobly toward) those who detest you and pursue you with hatred, invoke blessings upon and pray for the happiness of those who curse you, implore God's blessing (favor) upon those who abuse you [who revile, reproach, disparage, and high-handedly misuse you]. (Luke 6:27–28)

BE A "NOW" PERSON

Make a decision to be a person who lives each day in the joy of the Lord. Don't live in the past. Sometimes even the good things that have happened in the past hold us captive from receiving good things today if we dwell on them too long. Be a person who lives to enjoy the present—right now.

God wants you to have joy because great and mighty things are taking place in the lives of those who believe. There has not been, nor will there be, a day equal or parallel to this day. *Yesterday is gone forever, lost in the recesses of the past. Tomorrow has not yet arrived. So, live this day to the full.* Be a *now* person who is full of the joy of the Lord.

By now you should feel well prepared to keep your joy when the enemy tries to steal it from you. But the next chapter will show you why the Joy Stealer of jealousy also needs to be overcome.

TWELVE

Joy Stealer #6: Jealousy and Envy

———

Never compare yourself with anyone else because it invites covetousness, jealousy, and envy. This is one of God's commandments: "You shall not covet your neighbor's house, your neighbor's wife, or his manservant, or his maidservant, or his ox, or his donkey, or anything that is your neighbor's" (Exodus 20:17).

Coveting what others have is a big, big reason why people lose their joy. God wants His children to learn to love their own houses, their own spouses, their own gifts and abilities, their own positions and possessions—not someone else's.

"I wish I had her life."

"I wish I had his car."

"I wish I had their children."

"I wish I had a musical gift so I could be a worship leader and travel with a large ministry."

"I wish I was in a position of leadership where I could be the boss."

Does the commandment on the preceding page mean that it is wrong for us to want to have the same kinds of things other people have? No, there is nothing wrong with that. But we should never want what someone else has to the point that we become envious or jealous. These negative emotions poison our own lives and hinder loving relationships with others.

I try to refrain from looking at people and thinking things like, *Oh, I wish I looked like her. I wish I had hair like hers.* I have really fine, limp hair. I get it cut about every two weeks and keep it short because that seems to be the best hairstyle for my type of hair. I color it and bleach it and put everything I can find on it—mousse and gel and spritz and spray.

Our older daughter, Laura, has very thick hair. When she was growing up, she would get out of bed in the morning and fix it by turning her head upside down for a moment and running her fingers through her hair, and look gorgeous. My younger daughter, Sandra, and I would fix our hair by combing and spraying and spritzing, pulling and yelling—but Laura didn't have to do any of those things to have beautiful-looking hair.

Sometimes we women look at the models in magazines and feel very jealous and envious of their appearance. But most of those women don't look like that naturally.

You may disagree and say, "Oh, yes, they do. Those are actual pictures of those people."

I think those models are very beautiful, but magazines are known to touch up their pictures when necessary. And many of the models are teenagers whose skin looks like milk and honey and who have youthful figures. But after a woman has had a few babies, she doesn't usually look like that anymore.

When you get to be my age, some of the body parts that used to be high and firm have fallen low and flat. Some you can have lifted a little with surgery, but some things are just too far gone to be fixed.

So we look at all those beautiful, young girls on magazine covers, and we feel old, ugly, fat, and wrinkled. We feel so terrible that if we are not careful, we start to think, *I wish I looked like that. I hate those models.*

That kind of jealousy is found in the story of Joseph's coat, which was a special gift from his loving father, Israel.[1] The coat was very beautiful, and all Joseph's brothers were jealous of it. In fact, the Bible says that they hated him so much because of it, they planned to kill him. But then they decided to sell him into slavery. That is one of the more extreme results of jealousy, but it serves to remind us of how dangerous jealousy can be.

I encourage you to stop comparing yourself with other people in regard to how you look, what position you occupy, or anything else they have that you don't. Comparison only thwarts God's working in your life.

LOVE YOUR LIFE

Here is the problem: Covetousness, jealousy, and envy are not just saying, "I wish I had nice hair like hers," or "I wish I could lose weight as easily as that person can." These negative emotions can prevent people from loving someone who has what they want.

God puts gifts in people for the benefit of others: "All these [gifts, achievements, abilities] are inspired and brought to pass by one and the same [Holy] Spirit, Who apportions to each person individually [exactly] as He chooses" (1 Corinthians 12:11). Years ago, God began to reveal to me that when He puts a gift in someone to minister to me, if I am jealous or envious of that person's gift, then I cannot receive any benefit from it.

The only way we can receive what God has put in others for our benefit is by realizing that we don't have it and probably will never have it. God has gifted certain individuals and brought them into our lives so they can share their gifts with us and we can share our gifts with them. That is how the body of Christ works together to bless one another.

Let me give you an example. Maybe you can sew, and your neighbor can bake. Maybe you can't cook anything without burning it, and your neighbor can't sew a stitch. Instead of being jealous and envious of each other's gifts, you both can appreciate the fact that God put someone in your lives who has the gift you don't have so the two of you can complement each other.

You don't need to be covetous, jealous, or envious of others. God wants you to know that you are unique, and He has an individualized, specialized plan for you.[2] So learn to love your life.

JUDGE NOT

Being jealous of what people have causes us to judge them, which the Word clearly teaches is wrong: "Do not judge and criticize and condemn others, so that you may not be judged and criticized and condemned yourselves" (Matthew 7:1). Judgment comes out of pride; it causes gossip and all kinds of wrongs and is a big problem among believers today. The Bible has much to say about judging others. For instance, the King James Version of the verse above says, "Judge not, that ye be not judged." When we judge others for what they own—their houses, their cars, their jewelry, their clothes—it is usually because we are unhappy with what we have, not with what they have.

For example, if we are jealous of a person's car, then we may really be saying, "I'm not happy with my car, and I want your car."

Someone once gave me a brand-new car. Now, most people who saw me drive the car didn't know it was a gift. It was a sporty-looking car, and it was the kind of thing that a preacher could easily be judged for owning.

You might say, "I just wish somebody would give *me* a car."

I must admit, there have been times when I have heard about a blessing that someone has received, and I think, *When is that going to happen to me?* When that thought enters my mind, I immediately open my mouth and say, "I am happy for them. If God can do it for them, He can do it for me, too."

Instead of being unhappy or jealous or envious when God blesses someone with something we would like to have, we can be happy for them and let their blessing be an encouragement to us, believing that what God did for them, He can do for us. If He did it once, He can do it again.

Envying the blessings someone else receives will hinder your own blessings. Before you let yourself envy the blessings of others, ask yourself these questions:

- How hard am I willing to work in my life to get it?
- What kind of sacrifices am I willing to make?
- What am I willing to do to lay down my life to help somebody else as that person did?
- How many seeds am I willing to sow?
- Am I willing to give away what God tells me to give away?
- How much do I still have in my possession that God told me to give away a long time ago?

We always want what other people have, but we don't want to do what they had to do to get it. If we see a person's car and judge them for owning it, we may say, "I don't think she should have that car; I don't think that's a good testimony."

Could it be that it's not the fact that the person has the car that bothers us, but the fact that we don't? If we were driving one just like it, would we have a problem with that person's having it at all?

Suppose we look at a piece of clothing somebody else is

wearing and say, "I recognize that article, and I know what they paid for that. I don't think that's right. I don't think they should be spending that much money on clothes."

Would we care that they wore a particular garment if we had one like it? Would we care that somebody had a fur coat if we had one? Would we care that they had a diamond ring if we had one? Would we care that they had a big house if we had one?

If we are honest about the cause of the problem, we will find that most often we judge other people because we are not happy with what God is giving us. I believe God takes that personally, because if we are unhappy with what we have, we are really saying that we are dissatisfied with what He is doing in our lives.

You may ask, "But am I not supposed to want more than what I have now?"

Yes, you can pray and ask God for what you want. But you must trust Him and the timing in which He chooses to give it to you.

I wanted a lot of things a long time before I got them. I look back now and realize it is a good thing God didn't give me those things when I asked for them because that was the last thing I needed at the time.

Envy and jealousy will cause us to strive after things God will give us in His timing, if it is His will that we have them. Striving to change our situations or circumstances will only steal our joy.

Do you want to be joyful and extremely blessed?

When you begin to feel jealous or envious, be honest with God and ask Him to help you live free from it. Then replace those feelings of jealousy with your own promises from the Word of God, and trust Him to perform His good plan in your life until you see results. The next Joy Keeper will show you how to be so outrageously blessed you won't want anyone else's life but your own.

THIRTEEN

Joy Keeper #6: Be Outrageously Blessed

∽

You won't be tempted to covet what someone else has if you simply obey what the Lord tells *you* to do. Obedience will cause you to be radically and outrageously blessed! If you delight in God, He will give you the desires of your heart, just as these Scriptures promise:

> Delight yourself also in the Lord, and He will give you the desires and secret petitions of your heart. Commit your way to the Lord [roll and repose each care of your load on Him]; trust (lean on, rely on, and be confident) also in Him and He will bring it to pass. . . . Be still and rest in the Lord; wait for Him and patiently lean yourself upon Him; fret not yourself because of him who prospers in his way. . . . Those who wait and hope and look for the Lord [in the end] shall inherit the earth. (Psalm 37:4–5, 7, 9)

If you want outrageous blessings, you will have to learn to radically and outrageously obey whatever the Lord tells you to do.

To obey God, you have to know how to hear from Him. I do extensive teaching on this subject in my book *How to Hear from God,* but because hearing God's voice is so vital to experiencing true joy, I am going to repeat some of the foundations of this important principle of faith.

Before I explain what I mean by hearing from God, let me illustrate what happens when we *don't* listen to Him. The following story shows how we can tire ourselves and lose joy when we go our own way and do our own thing:

After this, Jesus let Himself be seen and revealed [Himself] again to the disciples, at the Sea of Tiberias. And He did it in this way: There were together Simon Peter, and Thomas, called the Twin, and Nathanael from Cana of Galilee, also the sons of Zebedee, and two others of His disciples.

Simon Peter said to them, I am going fishing! They said to him, And we are coming with you! So they went out and got into the boat, and *throughout that night they caught nothing.* (John 21:1–3, italics mine)

I like the King James version of verse 3 of this passage: "Simon Peter saith unto them, I go a-fishing." Has someone ever suggested something to you that sounded like such a good idea, your emotions jumped with enthusiasm to participate? Perhaps you said, "I go a-fishing with you!" I'm not trying to indicate that we need a divine word from God every time we make a move, but the Bible says we are to acknowledge God in *all our ways,* and He will make clear the way we should go.[1]

To acknowledge God basically means to care about what He thinks. We are supposed to live our lives in a way that shows we want to please God through our every action. Every day we need to submit our will to God. If you want to experience joy, I believe this should be a daily prayer:

> *God, I don't want to do anything today without You. If I try to do something that is not of You, I want You to warn me not to do it. Let me feel "a check," a hesitation, in my heart if what I am about to do is not in line with Your perfect will. I don't want Your permissive will, I don't want to be out of Your will, but I want Your perfect will in my life.*
>
> *Help me not to be stiff-necked, stubborn, or hardhearted. I've had enough of my own will. I've had enough experience to know that if I get my way and it's not what You want, it's going to turn out bad for me, God. So I'm willing to follow You, but please make my way clear.*

If you will pray something like this each day, I believe God will keep you in His will. We can't keep ourselves in the will of God without His help; the flesh is too strong. God knows how to lead us if we give Him permission to do so.

I was concerned about my strong disposition when I first learned how important it is to walk in the will of God. I was worried that no matter how much I wanted to follow Him, I would never be able to walk in His perfect will. But God showed me that if I would just pray and trust Him, He would take care of the rest. If I started to get off track, He would make sure I got back on track. I frequently told God I didn't want Him to let me get by with anything that wasn't His will.

The Word does not tell us whether or not a lot of things are God's best for us. If I'm praying for something that is not covered in the Word of God, I simply tell Him, "God, I want this. I'm praying for this, but I want Your will more than I want my own way. So, Lord, if it's not in Your timing, or if what I'm asking You for is really not what You want for me, then please don't give it to me."

I pray that way now because I tried my own way, and it didn't bring joy.

Jesus is the author and the finisher of our faith,[2] but we have to realize He is not obligated to finish anything He didn't plan for our lives. We start works of the flesh, "we go a-fishing," but there is no point in getting upset at God if He won't bless what He never told us to do in the first place. We need to learn to wait on Him and listen to what He is telling us to do—then simply obey Him.

Just like Peter's friends, we can get caught up in the emotion of the moment and jump into the middle of some seemingly great deal, but it will steal our joy and make us tired if the presence and the power of God are not there to bless it.

"Peter and the boys fished all night but caught nothing." What a message! When we go our own way, that's exactly what we catch—nothing! But the next verses show how important it is to hear and obey the Lord:

Morning was already breaking when Jesus came to the beach and stood there. However, the disciples did not know that it was Jesus. So Jesus said to them, Boys (children), You do not have any meat (fish), do you? [Have you caught anything to eat along with your bread?] They answered Him, No!

And He said to them, Cast the net on the right side of the boat and you will find [some]. So they cast the net, and now they were not able to haul it in for such a big catch (mass, quantity) of fish [was in it]. (John 21:4–6)

Fishing out of the will of God is equivalent to fishing on the wrong side of the boat.

Perhaps you have been struggling and striving and working and straining to make something happen; trying to make a plan work, trying to change things, trying to change yourself, trying to get your ministry started or make your ministry grow, trying to get more money, trying to get healed, trying to change or find a spouse. If you have been working and working and working with no results, God may be asking you, "Have you caught anything?"

If you are worn out after all your hard work, God may be telling you that you are fishing on the wrong side of the boat. Maybe you are out of God's timing—maybe you are out of His will completely.

If you have lost your joy, I suggest that you surrender your will to God, because He wants to radically bless you. Start by praying, "Lord, Your will be done and not mine."

BE READY TO OBEY GOD

Obeying God may lead you to do something you don't think you want to do. You will just have to trust that obedience will lead you to joy, because God always has your good in mind.[3]

Jesus asked Simon Peter, "Do you love Me more than these [others do—with reasoning, intentional, spiritual devotion, as one loves the Father]? He said to Him, Yes, Lord, You know that I love You [that I have deep, instinctive, personal affection for You, as for a close friend]. He said to him, Feed My lambs" (John 21:15).

If we love Jesus, the bottom line is that we are to do good things for others. Three times Jesus asked Peter if he loved Him, and each time Jesus said, "If you love Me, take care of those who follow Me."

In John 21:18, Jesus said to Peter, "I assure you, most solemnly I tell you, when you were young you girded yourself [put on your own belt or girdle] and you walked about wherever you pleased to go. But when you grow old you will stretch out your hands, and someone else will put a girdle around you and carry you where you do not wish to go." God challenged me with that Scripture by showing me that when we are new believers, we have our own plans and walk in our own ways. But as we surrender to God to really follow Him, there will be things He will ask us to do that we may not want to do—at first. But if we really love Him, we will let Him have His way in our lives.[4]

Are you in a position right now in which God is asking

you to do something you don't want to do? I strongly urge you to submit to Him; your joy depends on it.

I believe that to whatever degree we love Him, to that degree we will also obey Him. As our love for Jesus grows, our obedience becomes more radical. I'm more radically and outrageously in love with Jesus than I was when I first started this ministry. My love for the Lord grows just as my love for Dave has grown over the years we've been married. I certainly love Dave a whole lot more now than I did on our wedding day, and I know my love for him will continue to grow deeper.

I believe that as we obey God more, we will love Him more, and that obedience will bring such outrageous blessings, our love will grow deeper and deeper for Him. And to whatever degree we are obeying God, we can truly say that is the measure of our love for Him. As our love grows, our joy will abound.

I find that the more I love Jesus, the more self-control I have in my life. With more self-control, it is easier for me to say "No" to selfish desires and "Yes" to God, because "the love of Christ controls and urges and impels us" (2 Corinthians 5:14).

As our love grows for God, we won't want to offend Him. We won't want to grieve the Holy Spirit. We will just want to do what God wants us to do, and obedience will give us great joy.

Since Christ suffered in the flesh for us, for you, arm yourselves with the same thought and purpose [patiently to suffer rather than fail to please God]. For whoever has suffered in the flesh [having the mind of Christ] is done with [intentional] sin [has stopped pleasing himself and the world, and pleases God], so that he can no longer spend the rest of his natural life living by [his] human appetites and desires, but [he lives] for what God wills. (1 Peter 4:1–2)

God wants to speak to you, but it's not going to do Him any good if you're not ready to obey Him. Your flesh may suffer in order to obey God, but you won't walk in the will of God until you give up going your own way and let Him lead you to a place that He knows is better for you.

Arm yourself with the kind of thinking that says, *I would rather suffer than fail to please God.* If you surrender to Him, you will never again intentionally disobey God.

Be Ready to Hear God's Voice

Once you are willing to obey God, you must learn to listen for His instructions. From the beginning of time, God has talked to His people. Adam and Eve heard God's voice in the cool of the evening every day.[5] In the book of Revelation, we learn that John heard the voice of God while on the island of Patmos.

Saul, who became Paul, was on the Damascus road when the voice of the Lord came to him:

Saul, Saul, why are you persecuting Me [harassing, troubling, and molesting Me]? And Saul said, Who are You, Lord? And He said, I am Jesus, Whom you are persecuting. It is dangerous and it will turn out badly for you to keep kicking against the goad [to offer vain and perilous resistance]. Trembling and astonished he asked, Lord, what do You desire me to do? The Lord said to him, But arise and go into the city, and you will be told what you must do. (Acts 9:4–6)

The wonderful thing is that Saul responded right away: "Lord! What would You have me do?" That must be why God picked Saul to bring a revelation of grace to us. God picked one of the worst sinners He could find just to show us what grace really is. Saul was persecuting Christians when he first heard the Lord's voice; but the good thing about Saul was that as soon as Jesus brought correction to him, he submitted.

So how do we hear the voice of God?

God Speaks Through His Word

First, if you want to hear God's voice (His *rhema*), you have to study His written Word (His *logos*).[6] Any other way in which God speaks to you will always agree with His written Word.

The more knowledge you have of the logos (written) Word, the more God can speak a rhema (personal) word to you when you need it. In this way, He can speak to your heart by bringing to your remembrance specific Scriptures to answer the need you have. Or, while you are reading the Word, God may enlighten a Scripture so that you understand it in relationship to your situation. This is a common way God will speak to you.

The Bible says faith comes by hearing and hearing by the Word of God. The Amplified Bible translates that passage this way: "So faith comes by hearing [what is told], and what is heard comes by the preaching [of the message that came from the lips] of Christ (the Messiah Himself)" (Romans 10:17).

I was on an airplane one day and feeling hurt over a circumstance in which I had been treated unfairly. I felt down about it in my heart, but I opened my Bible, and Zechariah 9:12 immediately caught my attention: "Return to the stronghold [of security and prosperity], you prisoners of hope; even today do I declare that I will restore double your former prosperity to you."

My faith soared to a whole new level when I saw that. I knew God was saying to me that if I would not give up hope, and if I would have the right attitude, I would see the day when God would give me back "double" what was taken from me in that situation. And I have definitely seen that promise come to pass. It was only about one year later, almost to the day, when God did an outstanding thing to bless me.

If you want to hear the voice of God, I encourage you to love the written Word. Spend time reading it and storing it in your heart. Then when God gives you a Scripture, as He did me, you will know it is the Holy Spirit saying, "Here, this is for you."

When a Scripture comes to life for you and is full of sudden meaning, you need to hang on to it, because *that is God talking to you.* When your answers come through a prompting from God Himself, your faith will carry you through whatever trial is facing you.

GOD'S AUDIBLE VOICE

There is an audible voice of God, but He does not speak to us that way very often. There are references to God's audible voice in Daniel 4:31, and again in Matthew 3:17 at the baptism of Jesus. People do testify of hearing the audible voice of God, and I have heard God speak this way a few times in my life.

It is rare for God to speak this way, yet He is eager to talk to us through many other methods. I feel it is important to explain that most of the time when Christians say, "God spoke to me and said . . . ," they are talking about His still, small voice within their hearts.

First Kings 19:12 tells of a time Elijah needed to hear from God. God didn't speak through the earthquake or fire, but through a still, small voice. There are a lot of voices in the world, but the voice of God always speaks in agreement with His Word. His voice is full of wisdom and common sense, and leaves you filled with peace.

GOD SPEAKS THROUGH SUPERNATURAL INTERVENTIONS

In my book *How to Hear from God*, I share examples of how God sometimes uses prophecies, dreams, and visions to speak to His people.

I have had a few dreams in my life that I believe were prophetic, but most of my dreams are not messages from God. If a dream is from God, I believe you know immediately what He is trying to show you, or you soon get the interpretation of it.

For example, when I first began this ministry, I had a dream in which I was driving in a line of traffic when many cars suddenly stopped and parked on the side of the road, or found a place to turn around to avoid driving over a bridge that was submerged in water.

When I woke up, I sensed God's still, small voice saying to me, "Joyce, you're on a new journey. There will be times when the things ahead are going to look dangerous or unsafe, and you're going to be a little unsure." He said, "There are always going to be plenty of places in the road where you can park. There will be plenty of places where you can turn around, but I'm looking for someone who will go all the way through and do what I tell them to do."

When struggles came or things became hard, I remembered how God warned me in the beginning that I would be tempted to stop. Knowing that God had shown me in advance what I would face gave me the strength I needed to face the difficult times. Knowing that God was with me gave me joy.

I am grateful for prophecies and dreams that have confirmed things God has been leading me to know, but I also warn people not to seek prophecies from other people. Seek God and He will speak to you as He chooses.

And if someone says that God told them something about us, we should never try to *make happen* what they said would come to pass. A prophecy through someone else should bear witness in our hearts; it should agree with what God personally has been telling us. It should confirm something God has already revealed to us another way.

I have seen people get into horrendous messes because they make decisions based on what other people think God said about them. If someone brings us a prophecy, we should consider carefully the reliability of the one who claims to hear from God on our behalf, and we must also learn to hear from God ourselves.

In other words, don't quit your job just because someone says they believe you are to go to the mission field or to Bible college, unless *you know* that God told you to do this. You will lose your joy very quickly if you run from place to place without hearing from God yourself.

Most of the time God speaks through that "inner witness," or prompting of His Spirit, in our hearts. Romans 7:6 explains, "So now we serve not under [obedience to] the old code of written regulations, but [under obedience to *the promptings] of the Spirit* in newness [of life]" (italics mine). These promptings and our consciences let us know when something just isn't right. As Paul said, "I am speaking the truth in Christ. I am not lying; *my conscience [enlightened and prompted] by the Holy Spirit bearing witness with me"* (Romans 9:1, italics mine).

Remember, obedience to God's voice may not always be comfortable. You may feel God prompting you to apologize to someone you would rather ignore. He may speak to you and tell you to give away something you would rather keep. I know because He has challenged me to give away things many times. The joy that came from obeying Him was always greater than any pleasure I had in keeping something for myself.

You may be unsure that God is really speaking to you, and you won't find out if it is God until you do the thing He is prompting you to do. If it is God telling you to do something, you will feel joy once you obey Him. He will guide you through your conscience and keep you in perfect peace.

TAKE TIME TO BE STILL

While learning to recognize the voice of God, you must be willing to be wrong, or you will never find out what God can really do through you. You must also find times just to be still in order to hear God's leading in your life.

A busy, hurried, frantic, stressful lifestyle makes it very challenging to hear God.

Find a place to get quiet before God. Get alone with Him and tell Him that you need Him and want Him to teach you how to hear His voice. Ask Him to tell you what He has for your life. Ask Him what He wants you to do. Ask Him to show you what you are doing that He doesn't want you to do.

Present yourself to God, and listen. Even if you don't hear from Him, you will honor Him by seeking Him. He promises that if you seek Him, you will find Him—you will get a Word from God.

A woman told me that she had spent many hours praying and trying to get a Word from God. He never said one thing to her. Then two days later, as she was walking across her kitchen, God spoke to her as she reached for the refrigerator door. He gave her a clear answer to what she had been praying about before. She said, "Why didn't He answer me earlier?"

I honestly don't know why God sometimes waits to respond, but I do know that if we will be diligent to seek God, if we show Him that we want His will, He will speak to us. And to hear His voice, we must spend time listening for Him. "Your ears will hear a word behind you, saying, This is the way; walk in it" (Isaiah 30:21). It may not be in our timing, but God will speak to us and let us know the way we should go.

God will lead you by an inner knowing, by common sense, by wisdom, and by peace. As you wait for answers from God, concentrate on obeying Him in order to keep a clear conscience.[7] You will not have joy if you know God has told you to do something and you haven't obeyed.[8] But if you follow God's voice, you will be radically and outrageously blessed.

Even though you may be greatly blessed, if you allow habitual discontent to get a foothold in your life, you will still lose your joy. The next two chapters will show you what God's Word has to say about finding lasting contentment.

FOURTEEN

Joy Stealer #7:
Habitual Discontentment

~~~

We all are afflicted with discontentedness from time to time, but we must avoid habitual discontentment. A dissatisfied spirit robs us of joy and blinds us to seeing what God may be trying to teach us.

There will always be things we want to see happen in our lives, but we can learn to enjoy where we are on the way to where we are going.

Life is full of mountaintops and valleys. We go through periods where we are so thankful and think we are the most blessed people on the face of the earth. But if we're looking for it, we can find something to steal our contentment, and suddenly we are grumpy again. As long as we have a habit of being discontented, the Lord will keep repeating the same message to us, which is that contentment is God's will concerning us:

God's peace [shall be yours, that tranquil state of a soul assured of its salvation through Christ, and so fearing nothing from God and *being content with its earthly lot of whatever sort that is,* that peace] which transcends all understanding shall garrison and mount guard over your hearts and minds in Christ Jesus. (Philippians 4:7, italics mine)

I believe contentment is possible, no matter what our earthly lot is, and dissatisfaction can become a bad habit if we don't aggressively pursue joy.

AVOID REASONS TO BE DISCONTENTED

We can become discontented with God's timing when we are in a hurry but God isn't. And we can become discontented with ourselves; we always want to be something we are not or to be like someone we know.

It's important to learn to be happy with yourself because if you don't approve of yourself, you are never going to approve of anybody else. You can't give others something you don't have. Besides, you are never going to get away from yourself—you are with yourself all the time. So if you are discontented with yourself, just think of the lifetime of misery you have to look forward to.

If we say we love God, we should never want to do anything to insult Him or to grieve His Spirit; yet I believe our habitual discontentment is an insult to the Lord. When we become discontented and dissatisfied and show it by murmuring and grumbling, we are insulting the Lord. He says to us, "I'm in charge of your life—I've got a good plan for you, and I'm working out everything for your good. My ways are above your ways. My thoughts are above your thoughts. You may not understand what I'm doing, but trust Me."

He wants us to show that we trust Him. To trust God is to stop looking for reasons to be discontented.

ENJOY GOD'S BENEFITS

The kingdom of God offers benefits. One of those benefits is the privilege of being content and satisfied even when every circumstance in our lives doesn't necessarily suit us.

First Timothy 6:6–8 says:

> [And it is, indeed, a source of immense profit, for] godliness accompanied with contentment (that contentment which is a sense of inward sufficiency) is great and abundant gain. For we brought nothing into the world, and obviously we cannot take anything out of the world; but if we have food and clothing, with these we shall be content (satisfied).

I don't know many people who are satisfied with just food and clothing. Most of us have at least that, but there is still a lot of discontentment in people. This doesn't mean God is saying food and clothing are all He wants us to have. But He is saying that the basic necessities in life should be enough to make us happy.

I have preached in Third World nations where people don't live as well as the average American dog. I still shake my head in utter disbelief when I think of the way some people have to live in dirt with no decent water in which to take baths. They are hungry and have only rags to wear.

Every once in a while, we need a reality check to remind us of how little we need to still enjoy the kingdom benefits of contentment and satisfaction. It seems the Holy Ghost has to give us a tune-up so we will get back on track to contentment.

Consider the negatives of discontentedness. Habitual resentment leads to an unsatisfactory life. Constant feelings or displays of discontentment can be very distressing for you and those who know you. Being satisfied brings joy; being dissatisfied brings you torment.

It is easy (yet foolish) to get upset over something we can't do anything about. But that is usually what upsets us—something is out of our control. We would rather be little "Holy Ghost Juniors" and try to do what only God can do. We like to fix things to our instant satisfaction.

We want to fix our kids; we want to fix the people we work for and those who don't treat us right. We want to fix the world. We want to tell everybody how to do things, and we want them to get with it and do it *now*.

But the bottom line is, there are a whole lot of things only God can fix.

Be Joyful Today

Somewhere in the process of all this, we need to learn how to be content while we're on the way to where we're going. Otherwise, we will miss out on a lot of joy that is meant to be a kingdom benefit. We will never have this day back to relive. Once it's gone, it is gone forever. If we don't learn to enjoy this day, we will never have a second chance at enjoying it.

No wonder the psalmist King David commanded, "This is the day which the Lord has brought about; we will rejoice and be glad in it" (Psalm 118:24).

I have a feeling that when David got up that day, he was not feeling too perky. I think when we see positive confessions like this in the Bible, we are seeing a record of people who felt the same way we do most days, and they had to decide to make a faith statement about what they would do that had nothing to do with their feelings.

This day that the Lord has made is a commodity God has given to you—it is another day to live and breathe. What are you going to do with it? Will you rejoice and be glad? To do that, you may have to say to yourself, "I *will* rejoice in the day that the Lord has made!"

The positive side of contentment is very appealing. The word *content* denotes being satisfied with or resigned to your circumstances. That doesn't mean you have to accept what is going on in your life. It doesn't mean you'll never want change. I think it means to enjoy where you are on the way to where you are going.

Of course, we want changes for the better in ourselves, in our finances, and in the world and people around us. But while hoping for better days, the apostle Paul said that he had *learned* how to be content. He wrote:

I know how to be abased and live humbly in straitened circumstances, and I know also how to enjoy plenty and live in abundance. I have learned in any and all circumstances the secret of facing every situation, whether well-fed or going hungry, having a sufficiency and enough to spare or going without and being in want. *I have strength for all things in Christ* Who empowers me [I am ready for anything and equal to anything through Him Who infuses inner strength into me; I am self-sufficient in Christ's sufficiency]. (Philippians 4:12–13, italics mine)

Like Paul, we can learn to be satisfied to the point where we are not disturbed. We can still want change, but we can learn to be content whether we have a lot or a little. No matter what state we are in, Christ will empower us to be ready for anything. If we never become content with "a little," God won't promote us to "a lot."

I don't know how long it took Paul to learn contentment. I don't know how many times he had to go around the mountain before he learned that Christ was sufficient for all his needs whether he was rich or poor. But somehow, he finally learned to be content, and we can learn, too.

Problems come on days we don't want to have problems. We never get up and plan to have a problem. But we need to prepare ourselves for them because as long as we are on this side of heaven, problems will come our way. We need to pursue a deeper level of contentment and satisfaction in our lives.

Contentment is not going to just fall on us; we are going to have to go for it. We are going to have to learn to make decisions that result in contentment.

The New International Version of Paul's message is translated as:

> I am not saying this because I am in need, for I have learned to be content whatever the circumstances. I know what it is to be in need, and I know what it is to have plenty. I have learned *the secret of being content* in any and every situation, whether well fed or hungry, whether living in plenty or in want. I can do everything through him who gives me strength. (Philippians 4:11–13, italics mine)

ENDURE THE CONTENTMENT TESTS

Paul said he had learned the secret to contentment. Every situation he faced, whether well-fed or going hungry, he had strength for all things in Christ, who empowered him. He was ready for anything and equal to anything through Jesus, who infused Paul with "inner strength."

The previous verse has been used out of context so many times we have lost the real power of its message. People quote the verse, "I can do all things" and then become disappointed when they find they can't do what they wanted to do after all!

For example, you can't have a worldwide ministry just by

"wanting it badly enough." God has to call you and gift you for that. There are grace gifts in people's lives, and none of us can go beyond the call of God on our lives. Each one of us can reach the completeness of what God has called us to do—and that is where we will find the joy of contentment.

We can't simply say: "I'm going to do what you're doing, because *I can do all things* through Christ who strengthens me." I promise you that no matter how badly I may want to, I still could not lead worship. I am not gifted to do that!

In the early days of my ministry, I thought it would be especially "cool" if I could preach *and sing*. I even bought a guitar but soon realized my fingers were too short to bridge the chords. Now maybe some people who have little fingers like mine can still play a guitar, but I couldn't get mine to work.

I never learned how to read music, and nobody knows what key it is that I sing in! So, even if I say that I can do *all things* through Christ who strengthens me, I still can't lead you into a place of worship through my singing. I am not gifted that way, but I have learned to be content with the gifts I have and to enjoy the gifts God has put in others for my benefit.

Paul was saying in this verse that the secret to being content is the knowledge that, through Christ, we can endure whatever we need to endure. We can be happy when our circumstances aren't good, and we can also handle ourselves humbly when circumstances are good. It's important to be able to do both.

Finances can play a big part in a person's sense of contentment. But God told me there are two different tests people have to pass concerning money. He said that one test is how we act when we have money, and the other is how we act when we don't have any. Some people get a bad attitude when they don't have any money, but others can get a bad attitude when they do, if they allow money to make them feel as though they are better than everybody else.

Paul said that he learned to be satisfied with his circumstances, no matter what. His joy was not in material blessings. This is an important key to maintaining joy because as long as we are breathing on this earth, we are going to encounter a mixture of things we like and things we don't like. We are going to be surrounded by a mixture of people who make us feel warm all over and people who are difficult to be near.

BE BALANCED

God wants us to be content—no matter what. I was meditating on this secret to joy when the Lord showed me that we stay balanced by experiencing seasons full of gratitude during good times and seasons full of trust during times of trials. We need both.

First Peter 5:7–8 says:

Casting the whole of your care [all your anxieties, all your worries, all your concerns, once and for all] on Him, for He cares for you affectionately and cares about you watchfully. *Be well balanced* (temperate, sober of mind), be vigilant and cautious at all times; for that enemy of yours, the devil, roams around like a lion roaring [in fierce hunger], seeking someone to seize upon and devour. (italics mine)

We have a tendency to get out of balance, and when everything in our life is good, we become complacent. If our attitudes get bad, God will correct us. We don't have the ability to keep a right attitude if everything in our lives turns out just the way we want it to all the time. Pretty soon we get prideful and think our blessings are because we are so "spiritual."

When suddenly we are in a big mess, we realize how much we need God. We balance our blessings with humility and pray, "Oh, God, I need You. God, I am nothing without You. God, if You don't help me, I don't know what I'm going to do."

I recently had a minor surgery but ended up with major complications. I had pain as well as several other miserable symptoms for many days. I quickly gained compassion for sick people and committed to pray for them more frequently.

I also realized how foolish some of my previous complaining was. All I wanted at the time was for the pain and misery to go away; nothing else seemed important enough to complain about. Most of the things we complain about are minor when all things are considered. My trouble prepared me to handle my future good times with more compassion and thankfulness.

When something comes my way that I really don't like, I've learned to just pray, "God, I don't like this, but somewhere I must need this, and I believe that it's going to work out for my good. It may not feel good right now, but I believe some-where along the line it's going to work out for my good. And somewhere along the line it's going to fit into Your plan for my life."

Hold fast to contentment by believing that God's overall plan for you is good. His plan is not only to bless you, it's also to teach you to get through situations with the right godly attitude and to help you grow spiritually.

God wants us to be more than blessed. He wants us to mature and pursue holiness and consecration in order to live a sacrificial lifestyle that empowers us to be what God wants us to be. When you are balanced, you forget about yourself and become a blessing to others—that's when you experience real joy. The joy of *being* a blessing is greater than *receiving* blessings.

TIMES OF TESTING PASS

When I face difficult times, I tell myself, "This cannot last forever. This, too, shall pass."

You can probably look back at your life and see many dif-ficult times you have endured even though at the time you thought, *I cannot stand this for another day.* The devil prob-ably tempted you every five minutes to believe the trial was going to last forever.

As you consider how many times you have already made it to the other side of pain, you can be confident you will make it again through Christ, who strengthens you. And on the other side of trials, you will see how God turned those experiences into good for your life.

If you have been having problems for six months or more, it probably seems your problem has lasted for an eternity. But our years on earth are only a little drop of nothing compared to forever.

Paul knew that the seasons of trials pass. It is tough when we are going through trials, but Paul learned to keep his eyes on the prize of heaven and trusted God to prepare him so that God's glory was revealed through his life. He wrote:

> For our light, *momentary affliction* (this slight distress of the passing hour) is ever more and more abundantly *preparing and producing and achieving for us an ever-lasting weight of glory* [beyond all measure, excessively surpassing all comparisons and all calculations, a vast and transcendent glory and blessedness *never to cease!*], since we consider and look not to the things that are seen but to the things that are unseen; for the things that are visible are temporal (brief and fleeting), but the things that are invisible are deathless and ever-lasting. (2 Corinthians 4:17–18, italics mine)

When you are tempted to become discontented, remember: "This, too, shall pass." No matter how bad your current situation may look, God loves you. Never let go of the truth that God loves you, no matter what is going on in your life. You can trust that everything will work out good for you because God loves you.[1]

The people who have *real* problems are those who don't know Jesus. They have valid problems because they don't have hope.

As believers, we are more than conquerors because we have Jesus walking with us through our problems. Your

173

worst day with Jesus will be better than your best day without Him.

Make a decision to be content. Even when I was facing cancer, God told me, "Joyce, several times every day, I want you to say to Me, 'God, I love You. I know You love me. I trust You. I believe this is going to work out for good. All things work together for good.'"

I repeated those words so much that when I was waking up from the anesthesia, they told me I was saying, "All things work together for good for those who love God and are called according to His purpose. All things work together for good for those who love God and are called according to His purpose." And here I am, years later, alive and healthy and serving God.

Don't you know it makes the devil mad when he throws his best shot at us but we stay full of joy? No matter what he does, we can still say, "I love You, God. I trust You, and I know this is going to work out for my good."

SPEND TIME IN GOD'S PRESENCE

Keep the doorways open to contentment and satisfaction by right thinking and speaking, and by spending time with God. He will not let you be satisfied and content without Him.

There is a God-shaped hole inside every one of us, and we cannot buy something across the counter to fill that hole. The only thing that is going to fill that craving is God Himself. One prayer will not be enough. We have to have daily maintenance. The Bible says, "Ever be filled and stimulated with the [Holy] Spirit" (Ephesians 5:18).

I spent years trying to find a time to fit God into my day. God finally told me to stop trying to work Him into my schedule, but to work my schedule around Him.

Contentment is found in the Lord's presence.[2] The Psalms proclaim that the fullness of joy is in God's presence: "You will show me the path of life; in Your presence is fullness of joy, at Your right hand there are pleasures forevermore" (16:11). I love Psalm 17:15: "As for me, I will continue beholding Your face in righteousness (rightness, justice, and right standing with You); *I shall be fully satisfied*, when I awake [to find myself] beholding Your form [and having sweet communion with You]" (italics mine).

We will be fully satisfied when we awake to find ourselves beholding His form and having sweet communion with Him. When God is first in our lives to the point where He is the first thing on our minds when we wake up in the morning, we will have a depth of satisfaction that no devil can take away from us.

If you are ready to break the control of habitual discontentment in your life, I encourage you to pray this prayer:

Father, in Jesus' name, I take authority over the spirit of discontentment and dissatisfaction. I take authority over murmuring and grumbling and complaining, and I rebuke the evil spirits that work to bring these things into my life.

I pray for the anointing of the Holy Ghost to come on my mind and emotions. Fill me with Your Holy Spirit, with an attitude of thankfulness for what You've done in my life so that discontent will have no place to get into my thoughts.

Father, help me to stay on the narrow path that leads to joy in You. Amen!

As we learned with this Joy Stealer, discontentment robs us of enjoying many benefits that are available to believers, but the next Joy Keeper will show you contentment is something each of us can learn to have regardless of our circumstances.

FIFTEEN

Joy Keeper #7: Be Content

~~~

Contentment is a decision to be happy with what you already have. But I am convinced most people are not truly content. Unbelievers certainly aren't content, whether they realize it or not, but it is very sad how many believers have not learned to be truly content in their circumstances.

I wonder how many people can truthfully say, "I'm happy with my life. I love my spouse and my family. I like my job. I'm satisfied with my house and my car. There are things I want God to do for me, but I am content to wait until He does them in His timing. I do not covet anything that belongs to my neighbor. I am not jealous of anyone else or envious of what others have. If God gave it to them, then I want them to enjoy it."

The Word says, "Let your conduct be without covetousness; be content with such things as you have" (Hebrews 13:5 NKJV). I believe God actually tests us in this way. Until we can pass His "I-am-happy-for-you-because-you-are-blessed" test, we are never going to have any more than what we have right now.

Yes, God wants us to prosper in every way;[1] He wants people to see His goodness and how well He takes care of us. But we must desire God more than we desire His blessings. So He tests us to make sure this is the case before He releases greater material blessings into our lives.

There are times when God will run somebody in front of us who has exactly what we want—just to see if we can pass the test. God used to do that kind of thing to me, and at first I didn't understand what was going on. But I learned by experience.

Experience is so valuable. For one thing, when you get on the other side of it, you can look back and see how downright funny some of the circumstances really were that God allowed in order to test you. If you fight those experiences and rebuke the devil and try to get away from them, they will never do you any good. To get what you want from God, you must pass those tests.

My daughter Sandra once gave an exhortation about forgiveness. She told how she went through a situation with an individual who mistreated her and how it wasn't right for her to have to unfairly suffer that way. But she forgot to share that six months before this incident took place, she had said to me: "I'll tell you what I'm believing for this year, Mom. I'm believing to walk in love with every person I come in contact with, no matter how unlovely they are."

Now, when you pray a prayer like that, you had better buckle your seat belt and get ready because you are very likely going to be tested.

We pray all kinds of spiritual-sounding prayers, like "Oh, God, I want to walk in love. I want to live a self-sacrificing life. I surrender everything to You. Just do with me as You will." Then suddenly we find ourselves in a test that is meant to develop those characteristics in us, and we wonder what is happening.

Remember, if you don't want to go through a test, don't pray for those kinds of attributes—especially patience. One Greek translation of the word *patience* indicates that it is a fruit of the Spirit that is developed only under trial.[2] It cannot be obtained any other way.

How can we learn to be patient if we never have to endure anything we don't want to endure, put up with anyone we don't want to put up with, or go through anything we don't want to go through?

THE VALUE OF CONTENTMENT

The Bible teaches us to be content no matter what our circumstances may be. Paul wrote, "Not that I am implying that I was in any personal want, for I have learned how to be content (satisfied to the point where I am not disturbed or disquieted) in whatever state I am" (Philippians 4:11).

One dictionary defines the word *content* as "rest or quietness of the mind in the present condition; satisfaction which holds the mind in peace, restraining complaining, opposition, or further desire, and often implying a moderate degree of happiness."[3]

How to be content is something we all have to learn. It may take time, but you can begin by making a positive confession. Even if it is not true right now, say, "I am content."

It feels good just saying that, doesn't it?

If you continue to say you are content every day, it will be a great benefit and blessing to you. You may not realize it yet, but contentment is worth more than all the material possessions you could possibly accumulate in a lifetime. Nothing you have or will obtain is worth anything if you are not satisfied inside.

That's what the apostle Paul was referring to when he wrote in 1 Timothy 6:6, "[And it is, indeed, a source of immense profit, for] godliness accompanied with contentment (that contentment which is a sense of inward sufficiency) is great and abundant gain."

Remember, in Philippians 4:11–12 Paul talks about learning to be content. We usually learn to be content by living discontented lives for a long time and then saying, "Lord, I don't want to live this way any longer. Getting this thing or having that thing is not worth it. I don't want to be miserable anymore. Just give me what You want me to have because unless You want me to have it, I don't want it. From now on I'm not going to compare myself with anyone else. I'm not going to be jealous of anyone. I'm not going to be jealous of others in the church. I'm not going to be jealous of people who receive a promotion at work. I'm not going to be envious of anyone. I don't want what anyone else has. Lord, I want only what You want me to have."

Saying to God, "Lord, I want only what You want me to have," is the only way to peace and happiness.

What makes us unhappy? Seeing something we want— usually something somebody else has—and trying to get it for ourselves instead of trusting God to do what needs to be done in our lives. And I can prove it to you from the Word of God.

THE SECRET OF CONTENTMENT

What is James saying to us in the following passage?

> What leads to strife (discord and feuds) and how do conflicts (quarrels and fightings) originate among you? Do they not arise from your sensual desires that are ever warring in your bodily members?
>
> You are jealous and covet [what others have] and your desires go unfulfilled; [so] you become murderers. [To hate is to murder as far as your hearts are concerned.] You burn with envy and anger and you are not able to obtain [the gratification, the contentment, and the happiness that you seek], so you fight and war. You do not have, because you do not ask. (James 4:1–2)

I believe James is saying, "You stay upset all the time because you try to get all the things you want through your own efforts. You are never going to get them that way. You are just going to end up hating people and having bad relationships because you want what they have."

Then James summarized the whole situation in one sentence: "You do not have, because you do not ask." Essentially, he was referring to how we try to get things ourselves instead of asking God for them.[4]

You are probably thinking, *But I have asked God for things; He just hasn't given them to me.*

If you have asked God for something and He has not given it to you, it's not because He is holding out on you. It may be that either it is not His will, or it is not His time—or it may be that there is something better He wants to give you, but you are not yet spiritually mature enough to ask for it. Whatever the reason, it is never because He doesn't want you to be blessed.

You are God's child, and He loves you. He is a good God who does only good things,[5] and He wants to do for you so much more than you could possibly imagine.[6] But He loves you too much to give you things that are going to hurt you. He loves you too much to give you things that will ultimately make you more carnal or more fleshly or that may even drag you into sin because you are not yet ready to handle them.

If you are a parent, and you love your children, would you give them the keys to the family car before they were old enough to drive? Of course you wouldn't—because you know they might have a wreck and hurt themselves or others. God is the same way with His children. Because He loves us, He is not going to give us something before we have the spiritual maturity to handle it.

Many people use manipulation and worldly ways to get things they have no business having. And it's those very things that end up ruining them.

I have discovered that the secret of being content is to ask God for what I want and to know that if it is right, He will bring it to pass at the right time; if it is not right, He will do something much better than what I asked for.

ACCEPT GOD'S CHOICE

Strife, jealousy, envy, resentment, discontentment—all these things close the door to getting what you want.

It pays to be happy for others when they are blessed. If you can pass that test, you will find God's blessings coming into your life.

Being happy when someone else is promoted at work, in the church, or anywhere else will help you enjoy the good life God wants to give you.

In the following passage, we see 250 of the top leaders of the Israelites who were so jealous of Moses' position as the God-chosen, God-appointed leader that they rose up against him.

> Now Korah son of Izhar, the son of Kohath, the son of Levi, with Dathan and Abiram sons of Eliab, and On son of Peleth, sons of Reuben, took men, and they rose up before Moses, with certain of the Israelites, 250 princes or leaders of the congregation called to the assembly, men well known and of distinction. And they gathered together against Moses and Aaron, and said to them, [Enough of you!] You take too much upon yourselves, seeing that all the congregation is holy, every one of them, and the Lord is among them. Why then do you lift yourselves up above the assembly of the Lord? (Numbers 16:1–3)

Moses was God's choice. He didn't choose himself; God chose him. Yet those men came to Moses and said, "Who do you think you are, telling us what to do? Who do you

183

think you are, making yourself out to be the boss? All the Israelites are holy—every one of us. Why, then, do you lift yourself above us?"

The men were not really mad because Moses was the boss; they were mad because they were not the boss. They wanted Moses' position, so they couldn't like him. They were jealous of him, so they couldn't love him. They were envious of him, so they couldn't receive him as their leader.

So many people today don't like their bosses. You have to be a boss to understand that not everyone is always going to like you when you are in a position of leadership. It doesn't matter what you do or what kind of decision you make, somebody is not going to like you. There will always be someone who is going to complain and cause problems.

One big reason many people don't like their bosses is simple: They want to be the boss because they think they can do a better job of being in charge.

Actually, Satan may try to use someone like that to hinder and destroy a person in a leadership position. I have seen that happen in my own life.

CHECK YOUR ATTITUDE

I believe in treating my employees right. I feel that if I treat them well, they will want to work for me. For example, if I pay them well, they are not going to go out and look for another job.

Because I am good to my employees, I seldom have a problem with someone who works for me. But strife is one thing we will not put up with in our organization because it destroys the anointing.

The Word says, "Remind your people to submit to rulers and authorities, to obey them, and to be ready to do good in every way. Tell them not to speak evil of anyone, but to be peaceful and friendly, and always to show a gentle attitude toward everyone" (Titus 3:1–2 TEV).

I remember when I had to talk with someone in my employ who was causing problems. I finally had to tell that person, "I think the real problem here is that I'm the boss, and you're not. You may want to be, but you are never going to be the boss in this organization. So either change your ways and come under authority here, or you will have to find work somewhere else because this is not your ministry, and you are not going to run it." The person settled down quickly after that.

If you are not in a position of leadership in your job or in your church, you need to have a healthy attitude toward the people who are. With God, the attitude of the heart is everything. We can do what our bosses tell us to do while murmuring and grumbling behind their backs, but if we do that, we are not the kind of employees the Bible tells us to be. We may seem to get away with this attitude for a while, but we will not get our reward.[7]

Our reward comes from obeying the specific calling God has placed on our lives—not from trying to be like someone else or managing to accomplish great things as far as the world is concerned. God rewards those who follow an obedient lifestyle.[8] If we will just do what God is asking us to do and be the persons He made us to be, His rewards will literally chase us down and flood our lives.

185

BE YOURSELF

Moses was a smart man. He knew the problem these people were having. Do you see it? They didn't like their jobs:

> Moses said to Korah, Hear, I pray you, you sons of Levi: Does it seem but a small thing to you that the God of Israel has separated you from the congregation of Israel, to bring you near to Himself to do the service of the tabernacle of the Lord and to stand before the congregation to minister to them, and that He has brought you near to Him, and all your brethren the sons of Levi with you? Would you seek the priesthood also? (Numbers 16:8–10)

Levites had the honored positions of guardians and caretakers of the tabernacle,[9] but, as we see in this passage, they thought their jobs were too insignificant for them. So they complained to Moses, "All we do is take care of the temple, Moses, while you make all the decisions. Who do you think you are, being in charge of everything?"

Do you know what happened? The next day, Korah, Dathan, Abiram, their households, and the 250 leaders met with Moses and Aaron at the entrance to the tabernacle. Suddenly the ground split wide open, and Korah, Dathan, Abiram, their households, and all their belongings fell into the abyss. Afterward, the earth closed back over them. Then fire came forth from the Lord and devoured the 250 men.[10]

The same kind of situation occurred with Moses' sister Miriam and his brother Aaron. In Numbers 12:1 it is recorded that they rose up against Moses because they didn't like his choice of a wife: "Now Miriam and Aaron talked against Moses [their brother] because of his Cushite wife, for he had married a Cushite woman."

In the next verse we read: "And they said, Has the Lord indeed spoken only by Moses? Has He not spoken also by us? And the Lord heard it." In other words, they were saying, "Moses, do you think you are the only one who can hear from God?"

So it wasn't just Moses' choice of a wife that was bothering Miriam and Aaron. The thing bothering them the most was that they wanted to be in charge. But Moses was in charge, and they didn't like it.

Do you know what happened to Miriam? She came down with a quick case of leprosy.[11]

I wonder how many people have a type of leprosy (meaning any kind of problem) and live discontented lives simply because they are jealous or envious of other people. They don't understand that each one of us is an individual before God and that God has an individual plan for each of us.

Because of my background, I had many weaknesses in the area of accepting myself and being me. I was always comparing myself with others, jealous of them and their possessions and abilities. I wasn't being myself; I was trying to keep up with everyone else.

I often felt pressured and frustrated because I was operating outside my gifts and calling. When I finally realized that I could not do anything unless God had ordained it and anointed me to do it, I started relaxing and saying, "I am what I am. I cannot be anything unless God helps me. I am just going to concentrate on being the best me I can be."

God has made every one of us unique.[12] He personally made you and gave you gifts, talents, and abilities. Just think about it: Nobody else in the world is exactly like you. That means what is best for someone else may not be best for you.

So, when you are tempted to say to God, "I wish I looked like somebody else," or "I wish I could do this or that like them," don't say it. Be satisfied with who God made you to be. Remember that He made you exactly the way He wants you to be. If you try to be like someone else, you will miss the beautiful life God has planned specially for you.

Many people think they must become what another person is. That kind of thinking will steal our joy, and it's no one's fault but our own. We don't have to compare anything about our lives to another person's. All we're required to do is be who God created us to be.

It was so liberating to me when I finally discovered I did not have to be like anyone else. Before that, I thought I had to be like my husband, who has many wonderful qualities. I thought I had to be like my pastor's wife, and my next-door neighbor, and the lady at church who seemed to have it all together.

The psalmist wrote, "I am content and at peace. As a child lies quietly in its mother's arms, so my heart is quiet within me" (Psalm 131:2 TEV). Being satisfied and happy with yourself is a very important key to enjoying your life.

JOY IN SATISFACTION

You can have joy every single day by being satisfied with what you have and what you do. You don't need to want what others have or desire to do what they are doing. You don't need to be the boss or look like anyone else or live like anyone else. Always remember that if you had someone else's life, you would get not only the good parts but the bad ones, too.

You can find joy and say, "My soul shall be satisfied" (Psalm 63:5 KJV). If you've been struggling in this area, get a hold of yourself and say, "I am happy with what God is doing in my life. I don't want what anybody else has because I probably wouldn't be able to handle it if I had it. I only want what God wants me to have. I am going to ask Him for what I want and believe that He is going to give it to me, but only *if* it is right and *when* it is right for me to have it. Then I can have peace and joy."

Make a decision to stop being dissatisfied with what you think you don't have and give God what you do have. If you are a believer, you have wonderful things inside you. You can make somebody happy, lead someone to Christ, and encourage, edify, and exhort those around you. You can use your gifts and talents to serve God.

Whatever your situation, make the decision to trust God and be peaceful and content. No matter how much you may want to do what someone else is doing, or to have what they have, you will not be able to unless God wills it and strengthens you to accomplish it. He might have a different plan for you. Accepting that pays you great dividends

189

in the personal happiness and contentment that come from knowing you are in the will of God and enjoying the material blessings that He provides for you in accordance with the promises found in His Word.

God loves you and has designed only the best for you. Real contentment and joy come from remaining within the boundaries of what He has called and equipped you to do. Contentment and joy come from not trying to undertake things that aren't His will for you and, therefore, aren't within your God-given talents and abilities to accomplish. That is not negativism; it is godly wisdom.

Become content with the wonderful person God made you to be, and your joy level will improve dramatically.

SIXTEEN

You Can Live a Life of Joy

⟶

Joy is one of the most powerful weapons we have against the devil. He has evil intentions to destroy our lives, but joy is a great source of strength that God has given us to interrupt Satan's plan.[1]

Through joy, we overcome problems the devil will tell us are impossible to overcome and do things people would never believe we could do.

We can be defeated only if we lose our joy. The Bible says to "be joyful always" (1 Thessalonians 5:16 NIV).

Satan wants you down because he knows if you lose your joy, you will lose your strength, and if you lose your strength, he will walk all over you. But the Lord wants to lift you up,[2] and He does that through the joy of the Lord, which is your strength.[3]

It is not godly to be joyless all the time. *Matthew Henry's Concise Commentary on the Whole Bible* describes living a godly life as "a life of constant joy."[4] I believe to enjoy life that way is a gift of God.[5] But you will never enjoy your life if you don't believe it is God's will. Believing releases joy.

I was not raised in a joyful atmosphere. I was made to feel that if I was having fun, it was wrong. So I used to be down a lot. I worked hard and was a responsible person, but I did not really enjoy my life.

Satan robbed me of many things through my ignorance of God's Word. Because I lacked proper spiritual knowledge, for a while Satan deceived me and stole the victorious, joy-filled life Jesus had already provided in His plan for me. Now I live a life of joy because the Lord helped me to learn the things I have shared with you in this book.

The next time you feel as if you've lost your joy, I encourage you to get this book out because I believe you will find the reason you've lost your joy and how to get it back somewhere in these pages. We have looked at seven things Satan uses to steal our joy and what to do to overcome them. Joy is a fruit of the Spirit that dwells inside every believer's heart. However, it is released only by making a decision not to allow adverse circumstances to rule our emotional and mental attitudes.

No matter what happens in your life, remember this: You have the ability to release and maintain joy in your life, and there is nothing Satan can do to stop you when your heart is full of joy.

Scriptures on
How to Keep Your Joy

I encourage you to read the following Scripture passages, meditate on them, and confess them in faith and confidence on a regular basis. I believe they will help you fight off every attack the enemy, Satan, launches against you. Armed with the Word of God and the truths in this book, you will be able to do something awesome for yourself—stir up your joy and avoid the seven things that steal it.

> Be not grieved and depressed, for the joy of the Lord is your strength and stronghold.
> —Nehemiah 8:10

> A merry heart doeth good like a medicine.
> —Proverbs 17:22 KJV

> Rejoice in the Lord always [delight, gladden yourselves in Him]; again I say, Rejoice!
> —Philippians 4:4

This is the day which the LORD hath made; we will rejoice and be glad in it.

—Psalm 118:24 KJV

The thief comes only in order to steal and kill and destroy. I came that they may have and enjoy life, and have it in abundance (to the full, till it overflows).

—John 10:10

We who have believed (adhered to and trusted in and relied on God) do enter that rest.

—Hebrews 4:3

I have told you these things, so that in Me you may have [perfect] peace and confidence. In the world you have tribulation and trials and distress and frustration; but be of good cheer [take courage; be confident, certain, undaunted]! For I have overcome the world. [I have deprived it of power to harm you and have conquered it for you.]

—John 16:33

In [this] freedom Christ has made us free [and completely liberated us]; stand fast then, and do not be hampered and held ensnared and submit again to a yoke of slavery [which you have once put off].

—Galatians 5:1

[It is He] Who has qualified us [making us to be fit and worthy and sufficient] as ministers and dispensers of a new covenant [of salvation through Christ], not [ministers] of the letter (of legally written code) but of the Spirit; for the code [of the Law] kills, but the [Holy] Spirit makes alive.

—2 Corinthians 3:6

The law of the Lord is perfect, restoring the [whole] person; the testimony of the Lord is sure, making wise the simple.

—Psalm 19:7

I fear, lest somehow, as the serpent deceived Eve by his craftiness, so your minds may be corrupted from the simplicity that is in Christ.

—2 Corinthians 11:3 NKJV

Our boasting is this: the testimony of our conscience that we conducted ourselves in the world in simplicity and godly sincerity, not with fleshly wisdom but by the grace of God.

—2 Corinthians 1:12 NKJV

Lean on, trust in, and be confident in the Lord with all your heart and mind and do not rely on your own insight or understanding. In all your ways know, recognize, and acknowledge Him, and He will direct and make straight and plain your paths. Be not wise in your own eyes; reverently fear and worship the Lord and turn [entirely] away from evil. It shall be health to your nerves and sinews, and marrow and moistening to your bones.

—Proverbs 3:5–8

Dwell in Me, and I will dwell in you. [Live in Me, and I will live in you.] Just as no branch can bear fruit of itself without abiding in (being vitally united to) the vine, neither can you bear fruit unless you abide in Me. I am the Vine; you are the branches. Whoever lives in Me and I in him bears much (abundant) fruit. However, apart from Me [cut off from vital union with Me] you can do nothing.

—John 15:4–5

I resolved to know nothing (to be acquainted with nothing, to make a display of the knowledge of nothing, and to be conscious of nothing) among you except Jesus Christ (the Messiah) and Him crucified.

—1 Corinthians 2:2

God is not the author of confusion, but of peace.

—1 Corinthians 14:33 KJV

When angry, do not sin; do not ever let your wrath (your exasperation, your fury or indignation) last until the sun goes down. Leave no [such] room or foothold for the devil [give no opportunity to him].

—Ephesians 4:26–27

Understand [this], my beloved brethren. Let every man be quick to hear [a ready listener], slow to speak, slow to take offense and to get angry. For man's anger does not promote the righteousness God [wishes and requires].

—James 1:19–20

He who is slow to anger is better than the mighty, he who rules his [own] spirit than he who takes a city.

—Proverbs 16:32

Cease from anger and forsake wrath; fret not yourself—it tends only to evildoing. For evildoers shall be cut off, but those who wait and hope and look for the Lord [in the end] shall inherit the earth.

—Psalm 37:8–9

You shall not covet your neighbor's house, your neighbor's wife, or his manservant, or his maidservant, or his ox, or his donkey, or anything that is your neighbor's.

—Exodus 20:17

Do not judge and criticize and condemn others, so that you may not be judged and criticized and condemned yourselves.

—Matthew 7:1

Let your conduct be without covetousness; be content with such things as you have.

—Hebrews 13:5 NKJV

Not that I am implying that I was in any personal want, for I have learned how to be content (satisfied to the point where I am not disturbed or disquieted) in whatever state I am.

—Philippians 4:11

If we have food and clothing, with these we shall be content (satisfied).

—1 Timothy 6:8

I am content and at peace. As a child lies quietly in its mother's arms, so my heart is quiet within me.

—Psalm 131:2 TEV

My soul shall be satisfied.

—Psalm 63:5 KJV

Be joyful always.

—1 Thessalonians 5:16 TEV

Prayer for
a Personal Relationship
with the Lord

~

God wants you to receive His free gift of salvation. Jesus wants to save you and fill you with the Holy Spirit. If you have never invited Jesus, the Prince of Peace, to be your Lord and Savior, I invite you to do so now. Pray the following prayer, and if you are really sincere about it, you will experience a new life in Christ.

Father,

You loved the world so much, You gave Your only begotten Son to die for our sins, so that whoever believes in Him will not perish but have eternal life.

Your Word says we are saved by grace through faith as a gift from You. There is nothing we can do to earn salvation.

I believe and confess with my mouth that Jesus Christ is Your Son, the Savior of the world. I believe He died on the cross for me and bore all my sins, paying the price for them. I believe in my heart that You raised Jesus from the dead.

I ask You to forgive my sins. I confess Jesus as my Lord. According to Your Word, I am saved and will spend eternity with You! Thank You, Father. I am so grateful! In Jesus' name, amen.

(See John 3:16; Romans 10:9–10; 1 Corinthians 15:3–4; Ephesians 2:8–9; 1 John 1:9; 4:14–16; 5:1, 12–13.)

Notes

❧

INTRODUCTION
You Can Have Joy Every Day!

1. *American Dictionary of the English Language,* 1st ed. Facsimile of Noah Webster's 1828 edition, permission to reprint by G. & C. Merriam Company, copyright 1967 & 1995 (renewal) by Rosalie J. Slater, s.v. "joy."

2. "Therefore with joy will you draw water from the wells of salvation" (Isaiah 12:3); "My soul shall be joyful in my God" (Isaiah 61:10 NKJV); "In Your salvation how greatly shall he rejoice!" (Psalm 21:1 NKVJ); "Restore to me the joy of your salvation and grant me a willing spirit, to sustain me" (Psalm 51:12 NIV).

3. "For whatever a man sows, that and that only is what he will reap. For he who sows to his own flesh (lower nature, sensuality) will from the flesh reap decay and ruin and destruction, but he who sows to the Spirit will from the Spirit reap eternal life" (Galatians 6:7–8).

4. I cover this subject in more detail in my book *Enjoying Where You Are on the Way to Where You Are Going.*

CHAPTER ONE
Two Choices: Works or Grace?

1. "He gives us more and more grace (power of the Holy Spirit, to meet this evil tendency and all others fully). That is why He says, God sets Himself against the proud and haughty, but gives grace [continually] to the lowly (those who are humble enough to receive it)" (James 4:6).

2. "Those who honor me I will honor, but those who despise me will be disdained" (1 Samuel 2:30 NIV).

3. "The works of the flesh are manifest, which are these; Adultery, fornication, uncleanness, lasciviousness, idolatry, witchcraft, hatred, variance, emulations, wrath, strife, seditions, heresies, envyings, murders, drunkenness, revellings, and such like: of the which I tell you before, as I have also told you in time past, that they which do such things shall not inherit the kingdom of God" (Galatians 5:19–21 KJV).

4. "Now we, brethren, as Isaac was, are the children of promise. But as then he that was born after the flesh persecuted him that was born after the Spirit, even so it is now. Nevertheless what saith the scripture? Cast out the bondwoman and her son: for the son of the bondwoman shall not be heir with the son of the freewoman. So then, brethren, we are not children of the bondwoman, but of the free" (Galatians 4:28–31 KJV). (See also Hebrews 8:6–13; 9:1–28; 10:16–22.)

5. I cover the subject of marriage in more detail in my book *Help Me—I'm Married!*

6. "However, I am telling you nothing but the truth when I say it is profitable (good, expedient, advantageous) for you that I go away. Because if I do not go away, the Comforter (Counselor, Helper, Advocate, Intercessor, Strengthener, Standby) will not come to you [into close fellowship with you]; but if I go away, I will send Him to you [to be in close fellowship with you]" (John 16:7).

CHAPTER TWO
Joy Stealer #1: Works of the Flesh

1. "Who [with reason] despises the day of small things? For these seven shall rejoice when they see the plummet in the hand of Zerubbabel. [These seven] are the eyes of the Lord which run to and fro throughout the whole earth" (Zechariah 4:10); "His master said to him, Well done, you upright (honorable, admirable) and faithful servant! You have been faithful and trustworthy over a little; I will put you in charge of much. Enter into and share the joy (the delight, the blessedness) which your master enjoys" (Matthew 25:21).

2. "The fruit of the [Holy] Spirit [the work which His presence within accomplishes] is love, joy (gladness), peace, patience (an even temper, forbearance), kindness, goodness (benevolence), faithfulness, gentleness (meekness, humility), self-control (self-restraint, continence). Against such things there is no law [that can bring a charge]" (Galatians 5:22–23).

3. "Now there are distinctive varieties and distributions of endowments (gifts, extraordinary powers distinguishing certain Christians, due to the power of divine grace operating in their souls by the Holy Spirit) and they vary, but the [Holy] Spirit remains the same. And there are distinctive varieties of service and ministration, but it is the same Lord [Who is served]. And there are distinctive varieties of operation [of working to accomplish things], but it is the same God Who inspires and energizes them all in all. But to each one is given the manifestation of the [Holy] Spirit [the evidence, the spiritual illumination of the Spirit] for good and profit. To one is given in and through the [Holy] Spirit [the power to speak] a message of wisdom, and to another [the power to express] a word of knowledge and understanding according to the same [Holy] Spirit; to another [wonder-working] faith by the same [Holy] Spirit, to another the extraordinary powers of healing by the one Spirit; to another the

working of miracles, to another prophetic insight (the gift of interpreting the divine will and purpose); to another the ability to discern and distinguish between [the utterances of true] spirits [and false ones], to another various kinds of [unknown] tongues, to another the ability to interpret [such] tongues" (1 Corinthians 12:4–10).

4. This testing and proving "would reveal Abraham's faith as nothing else had done. He must give evidence of absolute obedience and unquestioning trust in Jehovah, must even obey blindly, proceeding step by step until the faith stood out as clearly as the noonday sun." *The Wycliffe Bible Commentary*, ed. Charles E. Pfeiffer and Everett F. Harrison, Electronic Database (Moody Press, copyright © 1962). All rights reserved.

5. "He said, Do not lay your hand on the lad or do anything to him; for now I know that you fear and revere God, since you have not held back from Me or begrudged giving Me your son, your only son. Then Abraham looked up and glanced around, and behold, behind him was a ram caught in a thicket by his horns. And Abraham went and took the ram and offered it up for a burnt offering and an ascending sacrifice instead of his son!" (Genesis 22:12–13).

6. "By tempting is not meant inciting to sin . . . but trying, proving, giving occasion for the development of his [Abraham's] faith." *Biblesoft's Jamieson, Fausset and Brown Commentary*, Electronic Database (copyright © 1997 by Biblesoft). All rights reserved.

7. "Let those who favor my righteous cause *and* have pleasure in my uprightness shout for joy and be glad and say continually, Let the Lord be magnified, Who takes pleasure in the prosperity of His servant" (Psalm 35:27).

8. See John 11:6–45. This passage tells the account of when Jesus' friend Lazarus died. In verse 15, Jesus explains, "And for

your sake I am glad that I was not there; *it will help you to believe (to trust and rely on Me)*" (italics mine). "When Jesus arrived, Mary, who had always had great faith in Jesus, ran to Him and said, "Lord, if You had been here, my brother would not have died" (v. 32). Then Jesus said to her, "Did I not tell you and promise you that if you would believe and rely on Me, you would see the glory of God?" (v. 40). Jesus then called Lazarus from the dead, and "upon seeing what Jesus had done, many of the Jews who had come with Mary believed in Him. [They trusted in Him and adhered to Him and relied on Him.]" (v. 45).

9. "Behold, I am the Lord, the God of all flesh; is there anything too hard for Me?" (Jeremiah 32:27).

10. See Genesis 3:1–13. Blame begins in verse 13: "And the Lord God said to the woman, What is this you have done? And the woman said, The serpent beguiled (cheated, outwitted, and deceived) me, and I ate."

11. "It was not the sneer of unbelief, but a smile of delight at the prospect of so improbable an event (Romans 4:20); he fully believed the word of God: there was humility blended with wonder and joy." *Biblesoft's Jamieson, Fausset and Brown Commentary*, s.v. "Genesis 17:17." See also Romans 4:18–21: "No unbelief or distrust made him waver (doubtingly question) concerning the promise of God, but he grew strong and was empowered by faith as he gave praise and glory to God. Fully satisfied and assured that God was able and mighty to keep His word and to do what He had promised" (vv. 20–21).

12. "Long delay seems to have weakened her [Sarah's] faith. Sarah treated the announcement as incredible, and, when taxed with the silent sneer, added falsehood to distrust. . . . In the circumstance of her incredulous smile, she was following the dictates of her natural reason only, not the word of God, whose power she limited by the results of her own observation and

experience." *Biblesoft's Jamieson, Fausset and Brown Commentary*, s.v. "Genesis 18:9–15."

CHAPTER THREE

Joy Keeper #1: Be Led of the Spirit

1. *Merriam-Webster's Collegiate Dictionary*, 11th ed., s.v. "acknowledge."

2. "For if I pray in an [unknown] tongue, my spirit [by the Holy Spirit within me] prays, but my mind is unproductive [it bears no fruit and helps nobody]. Then what am I to do? I will pray with my spirit [by the Holy Spirit that is within me], but I will also pray [intelligently] with my mind *and* understanding; I will sing with my spirit [by the Holy Spirit that is within me], but I will sing [intelligently] with my mind *and* understanding also" (1 Corinthians 14:14,15). "Pray at all times (on every occasion, in every season) in the Spirit, with all [manner of] prayer and entreaty. To that end keep alert and watch with strong purpose *and* perseverance, interceding in behalf of all the saints (God's consecrated people)" (Ephesians 6:18).

CHAPTER FOUR

Joy Stealer #2: Religious Legalism

1. "And it happened that the father of Publius was sick in bed with recurring attacks of fever and dysentery; and Paul went to see him, and after praying and laying his hands on him, he healed him" (Acts 28:8); "Then [the apostles] laid their hands on them one by one, and they received the Holy Spirit" (Acts 8:17); "You are in Him, made full and having come to fullness of life [in Christ you too are filled with the Godhead—Father, Son and Holy Spirit—and reach full spiritual stature]. And He is the Head of all rule and authority [of every angelic principality and power]" (Colossians 2:10).

2. Remember, grace is the power of God to help us in areas in which we cannot help ourselves.

3. "If it is by grace (His unmerited favor and graciousness), it is no longer conditioned on works or anything men have done. Otherwise, grace would no longer be grace [it would be meaningless]" (Romans 11:6).

4. *Matthew Henry's Commentary on the Whole Bible: New Modern Edition*, Electronic Database (copyright © 1991 by Hendrickson Publishers, Inc.). Used by permission. All rights reserved, s.v. "John 9:13–34."

5. "Therefore, [inheriting] the promise is the outcome of faith and depends [entirely] on faith, in order that it might be given as an act of grace (unmerited favor), to make it stable and valid and guaranteed to all his descendants—not only to the devotees and adherents of the Law, but also to those who share the faith of Abraham, who is [thus] the father of us all" (Romans 4:16).

6. "The thief comes only in order to steal and kill and destroy. I came that they may have and enjoy life, and have it in abundance (to the full, till it overflows)" (John 10:10).

7. "For the kingdom of God is not meat and drink; but righteousness, and peace, and joy in the Holy Ghost" (Romans 14:17 KJV).

CHAPTER FIVE
Joy Keeper #2: Be Free in Christ

1. "To whom did He swear that they should not enter His rest, but to those who disobeyed [who had not listened to His word and who refused to be compliant or be persuaded]?" (Hebrews 3:18).

2. "In [this] freedom Christ has made us free [and completely liberated us]; stand fast then, and do not be hampered and held ensnared and submit again to a yoke of slavery [which you have once put off]" (Galatians 5:1).

CHAPTER SIX
Joy Stealer #3: Complicating Simple Issues

1. "A man's mind plans his way, but the Lord directs his steps and makes them sure" (Proverbs 16:9); "Man's steps are ordered by the Lord. How then can a man understand his way?" (Proverbs 20:24); "O Lord [pleads Jeremiah in the name of the people], I know that [the determination of] the way of a man is not in himself; it is not in man [even in a strong man or in a man at his best] to direct his [own] steps" (Jeremiah 10:23).

2. "Jesus said unto him, If thou canst believe, all things are possible to him that believeth" (Mark 9:23 KJV); "But to as many as did receive and welcome Him, He gave the authority (power, privilege, right) to become the children of God, that is, to those who believe in (adhere to, trust in, and rely on) His name" (John 1:12); "For God so loved the world, that he gave his only begotten Son, that whosoever believeth in him should not perish, but have everlasting life" (John 3:16 KJV).

3. Jesus said, "Truly I say to you, unless you repent (change, turn about) and become like little children [trusting, lowly, loving, forgiving], you can never enter the kingdom of heaven [at all]. Whoever will humble himself therefore and become like this little child [trusting, lowly, loving, forgiving] is greatest in the kingdom of heaven" (Matthew 18:3–4).

4. "Now there was a certain man among the Pharisees named Nicodemus, a ruler (a leader, an authority) among the Jews, who came to Jesus at night and said to Him, Rabbi, we know and are certain that You have come from God [as] a Teacher; for no one can do these signs (these wonderworks, these miracles—and produce the proofs) that You do unless God is with him" (John 3:1–2).

5. "[Remember] this: he who sows sparingly and grudgingly will also reap sparingly and grudgingly, and he who sows gener-

ously [that blessings may come to someone] will also reap generously and with blessings" (2 Corinthians 9:6).

6. "For if you forgive people their trespasses [their reckless and willful sins, leaving them, letting them go, and giving up resentment], your heavenly Father will also forgive you" (Matthew 6:14).

7. "But I tell you, Love your enemies and pray for those who persecute you" (Matthew 5:44).

8. "As it is written: 'I have made you a father of many nations.' He is our father in the sight of God, in whom he believed—the God who gives life to the dead and calls things that are not as though they were" (Romans 4:17 NIV).

9. "But blessed is the man who trusts in the LORD, whose confidence is in him" (Jeremiah 17:7 NIV);"But seek first his kingdom and his righteousness, and all these things will be given to you as well" (Matthew 6:33 NIV).

CHAPTER SEVEN

Joy Keeper #3: Be Uncomplicated

1. "For after that in the wisdom of God the world by wisdom knew not God, it pleased God by the foolishness of preaching to save them that believe" (1 Corinthians 1:21 KJV).

2. "The mighty One, God, the Lord, speaks and calls the earth from the rising of the sun to its setting" (Psalm 50:1); "Have we not all one Father? Has not one God created us? Why then do we deal faithlessly and treacherously each against his brother, profaning the covenant of [God with] our fathers?" (Malachi 2:10).

3. *Merriam-Webster's Collegiate Dictionary*, 11th ed.

4. Ibid.

5. "When you pray, do not heap up phrases (multiply words, repeating the same ones over and over) as the Gentiles do, for

they think they will be heard for their much speaking. Do not be like them, for your Father knows what you need before you ask Him" (Matthew 6:7–8).

CHAPTER EIGHT
Joy Stealer #4: Excessive Reasoning

1. "While the earth remains, seedtime and harvest, cold and heat, summer and winter, and day and night shall not cease" (Genesis 8:22); "[Remember] this: he who sows sparingly and grudgingly will also reap sparingly and grudgingly, and he who sows generously [that blessings may come to someone] will also reap generously and with blessings" (2 Corinthians 9:6).

2. "I have told you all this so that you will have peace of heart and mind. Here on earth you will have many trials and sorrows; but cheer up, for I have overcome the world" (John 16:33 TLB).

3. "Those who live according to the sinful nature have their minds set on what that nature desires; but those who live in accordance with the Spirit have their minds set on what the Spirit desires. The mind of sinful man is death, but the mind controlled by the Spirit is life and peace" (Romans 8:5–6 NIV).

4. "The peace of God, which passeth all understanding, shall keep your hearts and minds through Christ Jesus" (Philippians 4:7 KJV).

5. "Whom having not seen, ye love; in whom, though now ye see him not, yet believing, ye rejoice with joy unspeakable and full of glory" (1 Peter 1:8 KJV).

6. "Now unto him that is able to do exceeding abundantly above all that we ask or think, according to the power that worketh in us . . ." (Ephesians 3:20 KJV).

7. See Acts 9:3–8 NIV: "Suddenly a light from heaven flashed around him. He fell to the ground and heard a voice say to him, 'Saul, Saul, why do you persecute me?' 'Who are you, Lord?'

Saul asked. 'I am Jesus, whom you are persecuting,' he replied" (vv. 3–5).

8. "You shall not bow down yourself to them or serve them; for I the Lord your God am a jealous God, visiting the iniquity of the fathers upon the children to the third and fourth generation of those who hate Me" (Exodus 20:5).

9. Albert Barnes, *Barnes' Notes*, Electronic Database (copyright © 1997 by Biblesoft). All rights reserved, s.v. "Psalm 127:1."

10. "If a blind man leads a blind man, both will fall into a ditch. But Peter said to Him, Explain this proverb (this maxim) to us. And He said, Are you also even yet dull and ignorant [without understanding and unable to put things together]?" (Matthew 15:14–16); "He kept repeating, Do you not yet understand?" (Mark 8:21).

11. "Be strong, courageous, and firm; fear not nor be in terror before them, for it is the Lord your God Who goes with you; He will not fail you or forsake you. . . . It is the Lord Who goes before you; He will [march] with you; He will not fail you or let you go or forsake you; [let there be no cowardice or flinching, but] fear not, neither become broken [in spirit] (depressed, dismayed, and unnerved with alarm)" (Deuteronomy 31:6, 8).

12. "For no temptation (no trial regarded as enticing to sin), [no matter how it comes or where it leads] has overtaken you and laid hold on you that is not common to man [that is, no temptation or trial has come to you that is beyond human resistance and that is not adjusted and adapted and belonging to human experience, and such as man can bear]. But God is faithful [to His Word and to His compassionate nature], and He [can be trusted] not to let you be tempted and tried and assayed beyond your ability and strength of resistance and power to endure, but with the temptation He will [always] also provide the way out (the means of escape to a landing place), that you may be capable and strong and powerful to bear up under it patiently"

(1 Corinthians 10:13); "Faithful is He Who is calling you [to Himself] and utterly trustworthy, and He will also do it [fulfill His call by hallowing and keeping you]" (1 Thessalonians 5:24); "So let us seize and hold fast and retain without wavering the hope we cherish and confess and our acknowledgement of it, for He Who promised is reliable (sure) and faithful to His word" (Hebrews 10:23).

CHAPTER NINE
Joy Keeper #4: Be Confident in God

1. "Though for myself I have [at least grounds] to rely on the flesh. If any other man considers that he has or seems to have reason to rely on the flesh and his physical and outward advantages, I have still more! Circumcised when I was eight days old, of the race of Israel, of the tribe of Benjamin, a Hebrew [and the son] of Hebrews; as to the observance of the Law I was of [the party of] the Pharisees, as to my zeal, I was a persecutor of the church, and by the Law's standard of righteousness (supposed justice, uprightness, and right standing with God) I was proven to be blameless and no fault was found with me" (Philippians 3:4–6).

2. "For whoever keeps the whole law and yet stumbles at just one point is guilty of breaking all of it" (James 2:10 NIV).

3. "You want something but don't get it. You kill and covet, but you cannot have what you want. You quarrel and fight. You do not have, because you do not ask God" (James 4:2 NIV).

CHAPTER TEN
Joy Stealer #5: Ungodly Anger

1. "The thief comes only in order to steal and kill and destroy. I came that they may have and enjoy life, and have it in abundance (to the full, till it overflows)" (John 10:10); "Leave no [such] room or foothold for the devil [give no opportunity to him]" (Ephesians 4:27).

2. "For we know Him Who said, Vengeance is Mine [retribution and the meting out of full justice rest with Me]; I will repay [I will exact the compensation], says the Lord. And again, The Lord will judge and determine and solve and settle the cause and the cases of His people" (Hebrews 10:30).

3. "For we are not wrestling with flesh and blood [contending only with physical opponents], but against the despotisms, against the powers, against [the master spirits who are] the world rulers of this present darkness, against the spirit forces of wickedness in the heavenly (supernatural) sphere" (Ephesians 6:12).

4. Righteousness is right actions; it is knowing you are right with God.

5. If you would like to learn more about dealing with anger, you can order my tape series called How to Handle & Deal with Anger, by writing to my office or visiting my Web site.

6. "But He said to me, My grace (My favor and loving-kindness and mercy) is enough for you [sufficient against any danger and enables you to bear the trouble manfully]; for My strength and power are made perfect (fulfilled and completed) and show themselves most effective in [your] weakness" (2 Corinthians 12:9).

7. "The fruit of the Spirit is love, joy, peace, patience, kindness, goodness, faithfulness, gentleness and self-control. Against such things there is no law" (Galatians 5:22–23 NIV); "For you were once darkness, but now you are light in the Lord. Live as children of light (for the fruit of the light consists in all goodness, righteousness and truth) and find out what pleases the Lord" (Ephesians 5:8–10 NIV).

8. "Then [Ezra] told them, Go your way, eat the fat, drink the sweet drink, and send portions to him for whom nothing is prepared; for this day is holy to our Lord. And be not grieved and depressed, for the joy of the Lord is your strength and stronghold" (Nehemiah 8:10).

9. "Therefore be imitators of God [copy Him and follow His example], as well-beloved children [imitate their father]" (Ephesians 5:1).

10. Adam Clarke, *Clarke's Commentary*, Electronic Database (copyright © 1996 by Biblesoft). All rights reserved, s.v. "Genesis 1:26."

11. "Give, and it will be given to you. A good measure, pressed down, shaken together and running over, will be poured into your lap. For with the measure you use, it will be measured to you" (Luke 6:38 NIV).

12. Robert Andrews, Mary Biggs, and Michal Seidel, et al., *The Columbia World of Quotations* (New York: Columbia University Press, 1996), s.v. "Alexander Pope," http://www.bartleby.com/66/9/44909.html.

13. "For as you know him better, he will give you, through his great power, everything you need for living a truly good life: he even shares his own glory and his own goodness with us! And by that same mighty power he has given us all the other rich and wonderful blessings he promised; for instance, the promise to save us from the lust and rottenness all around us, and to give us his own character" (2 Peter 1:3–4 TLB).

14. "But none of these things move me; neither do I esteem my life dear to myself, if only I may finish my course with joy and the ministry which I have obtained from [which was entrusted to me by] the Lord Jesus, faithfully to attest to the good news (Gospel) of God's grace (His unmerited favor, spiritual blessing, and mercy)" (Acts 20:24).

CHAPTER ELEVEN
Joy Keeper #5: Be Quick to Forgive

1. "As far as the east is from the west, so far hath he removed our transgressions from us" (Psalm 103:12 KJV).

2. "I, even I, *am he who blots out your transgressions*, for my own sake, and remembers your sins no more" (Isaiah 43:25 NIV, italics mine).

3. "1. LOGOS denotes (I) the expression of thought; 2. RHEMA denotes that which is spoken, "The significance of *rhema* (as distinct from logos is exemplified in the injunction to take "the sword of the Spirit, which is the word of God," Eph. 6:17; here the reference is not to the whole Bible as such, but to the individual scripture which the Spirit brings to our remembrance for use in time of need, a prerequisite being the regular storing of the mind with Scripture." W. E. Vine, *An Expository Dictionary of New Testament Words* (Old Tappan, NJ: Fleming H. Revell).

4. "Without faith it is impossible to please and be satisfactory to Him. For whoever would come near to God must [necessarily] believe that God exists and that He is the rewarder of those who earnestly and diligently seek Him [out]" (Hebrews 11:6).

5. *Merriam-Webster's Collegiate Dictionary*, 11th ed.

6. "Casting down imaginations, and every high thing that exalteth itself against the knowledge of God, and bringing into captivity every thought to the obedience of Christ" (2 Corinthians 10:5 KJV).

7. "Then Peter came up to Him and said, Lord, how many times may my brother sin against me and I forgive him and let it go? [As many as] up to seven times?" (Matthew 18:21).

8. "Not by might, nor by power, but by My Spirit [of Whom the oil is a symbol], says the Lord of hosts" (Zechariah 4:6).

CHAPTER TWELVE
Joy Stealer #6: Jealousy and Envy

1. "Now Israel loved Joseph more than all his children, because he was the son of his old age: and he made him a coat of many

colours. And when his brethren saw that their father loved him more than all his brethren, they hated him, and could not speak peaceably unto him" (Genesis 37:3–4 KJV).

2. "For I know the plans I have for you," declares the LORD, "plans to prosper you and not to harm you, plans to give you hope and a future" (Jeremiah 29:11).

CHAPTER THIRTEEN
Joy Keeper #6: Be Outrageously Blessed

1. "In all your ways acknowledge him, and he will make your paths straight" (Proverbs 3:6 NIV).

2. "Let us fix our eyes on Jesus, the author and perfecter of our faith, who for the joy set before him endured the cross, scorning its shame, and sat down at the right hand of the throne of God" (Hebrews 12:2 NIV).

3. "We are assured and know that [God being a partner in their labor] all things work together and are [fitting into a plan] for good to and for those who love God and are called according to [His] design and purpose" (Romans 8:28).

4. "If you [really] love Me, you will keep (obey) My commands" (John 14:15).

5. "They heard the voice of the LORD God walking in the garden in the cool of the day: and Adam and his wife hid themselves from the presence of the LORD God amongst the trees of the garden" (Genesis 3:8 KJV).

6. "1. LOGOS denotes (I) the expression of thought; 2. RHEMA denotes that which is spoken, "The significance of *rhema* (as distinct from logos is exemplified in the injunction to take "the sword of the Spirit, which is the word of God," Eph. 6:17; here the reference is not to the whole Bible as such, but

to the individual scripture which the Spirit brings to our remembrance for use in time of need, a prerequisite being the regular storing of the mind with Scripture." (Vine, *An Expository Dictionary*).

7. "Therefore I always exercise and discipline myself [mortifying my body, deadening my carnal affections, bodily appetites, and worldly desires, endeavoring in all respects] to have a clear (unshaken, blameless) conscience, void of offense toward God and toward men" (Acts 24:16).

8. "Let the peace (soul harmony which comes) from Christ rule (act as umpire continually) in your hearts [deciding and settling with finality all questions that arise in your minds, in that peaceful state] to which as [members of Christ's] one body you were also called [to live]. And be thankful (appreciative), [giving praise to God always]" (Colossians 3:15).

CHAPTER FOURTEEN
Joy Stealer #7: Habitual Discontentment

1. "Who shall ever separate us from Christ's love? Shall suffering and affliction and tribulation? Or calamity and distress? Or persecution or hunger or destitution or peril or sword? Even as it is written, For Thy sake we are put to death all the day long; we are regarded and counted as sheep for the slaughter. Yet amid all these things we are more than conquerors and gain a surpassing victory through Him Who loved us" (Romans 8:35–37).

2. "One thing have I asked of the Lord, that will I seek, inquire, for, and [insistently] require: that I may dwell in the house of the Lord [in His presence] all the days of my life" (Psalm 27:4).

CHAPTER FIFTEEN
Joy Keeper #7: Be Content

1. "Beloved, I pray that you may prosper in every way and [that your body] may keep well, even as [I know] your soul keeps well and prospers" (3 John 1:2).

2. "I. HUPOMONE . . . endurance, as, (a) in trials . . . (c) under chastisement, which is trial viewed as coming from the hand of God our Father" (Vine, *An Expository Dictionary*, pp. 167–68, s.v. "patience, patient, patiently, A. Nouns.")

3. Webster's 1828 edition, s.v. "content."

4. "One reason their desires . . . were not being realized was that they did not ask God, Who alone can fully satisfy human desires. A second reason is found in the unacceptable motive of those who do ask—*that ye may consume it upon your lusts*" (James 4:3 KJV). The essential condition of all prayer is found in 1 John 5:14 (KJV): *"If we ask any thing according to his will, he heareth us." The Wycliffe Bible Commentary*, s.v. "James 4:2–3."

5. "If you then, evil as you are, know how to give good and advantageous gifts to your children, how much more will your Father Who is in heaven [perfect as He is] give good and advantageous things to those who keep on asking Him!" (Matthew 7:11).

6. "Now to Him Who, by (in consequence of) the [action of His] power that is at work within us, is able to [carry out His purpose and] do superabundantly, far over and above all that we [dare] ask or think [infinitely beyond our highest prayers, desires, thoughts, hopes, or dreams]" (Ephesians 3:20).

7. "Servants, be obedient to them that are your masters according to the flesh, with fear and trembling, in singleness of your heart, as unto Christ; not with eyeservice, as menpleasers; but as the servants of Christ, doing the will of God from the heart; with

good will doing service, as to the Lord, and not to men: Knowing that whatsoever good thing any man doeth, the same shall he receive of the Lord, whether he be bond or free" (Ephesians 6:5–8 KJV).

8. "If thou shalt hearken diligently unto the voice of the LORD thy God, to observe and to do all his commandments which I command thee this day, that the LORD thy God will set thee on high above all nations of the earth: And all these blessings shall come on thee. . . . Blessed shalt thou be in the city, and blessed shalt thou be in the field. Blessed shall be the fruit of thy body, and the fruit of thy ground, and the fruit of thy cattle, the increase of thy kine, and the flocks of thy sheep. Blessed shall be thy basket and thy store. Blessed shalt thou be when thou comest in, and blessed shalt thou be when thou goest out. The LORD shall cause thine enemies that rise up against thee to be smitten before thy face. . . . The LORD shall command the blessing upon thee in thy storehouses, and in all that thou settest thine hand unto. . . . The LORD shall establish thee an holy people unto himself, as he hath sworn unto thee, if thou shalt keep the commandments of the LORD thy God, and walk in his ways. . . . And the LORD shall make thee plenteous in goods, in the fruit of thy body, and in the fruit of thy cattle, and in the fruit of thy ground. . . . The LORD shall open unto thee his good treasure, the heaven to give the rain unto thy land in his season, and to bless all the work of thine hand: and thou shalt lend unto many nations, and thou shalt not borrow. And the LORD shall make thee the head, and not the tail; and thou shalt be above only, and thou shalt not be beneath; if that thou hearken unto the commandments of the LORD thy God, which I command thee this day, to observe and to do them: And thou shalt not go aside from any of the words which I command thee this day, to the right hand, or to the left, to go after other gods to serve them" (Deuteronomy 28:1–14 KJV).

9. "The Levites shall pitch round about the tabernacle of testimony, that there be no wrath upon the congregation of the chil-

dren of Israel: and the Levites shall keep the charge of the tabernacle of testimony" (Numbers 1:53 KJV).

10. "There came out a fire from the LORD, and consumed the two hundred and fifty men that offered incense" (Numbers 16:35 KJV).

11. "The anger of the LORD was kindled against them; and he departed. And the cloud departed from off the tabernacle; and, behold, Miriam became leprous, white as snow: and Aaron looked upon Miriam, and, behold, she was leprous. And Aaron said unto Moses, Alas, my lord, I beseech thee, lay not the sin upon us, wherein we have done foolishly, and wherein we have sinned. Let her not be as one dead, of whom the flesh is half consumed when he cometh out of his mother's womb. And Moses cried unto the LORD, saying, Heal her now, O God, I beseech thee. And the LORD said unto Moses, If her father had but spit in her face, should she not be ashamed seven days? let her be shut out from the camp seven days, and after that let her be received in again. And Miriam was shut out from the camp seven days: and the people journeyed not till Miriam was brought in again" (Numbers 12:9–15 KJV).

12. "For You formed my inward parts; You covered me in my mother's womb. I will praise You, for I am fearfully and wonderfully made; marvelous are Your works, and that my soul knows very well. My frame was not hidden from You, when I was made in secret, and skillfully wrought in the lowest parts of the earth. Your eyes saw my substance, being yet unformed. And in Your book they all were written, the days fashioned for me, when as yet there were none of them" (Psalm 139:13–16).

CHAPTER SIXTEEN
You Can Live a Life of Joy

1. "The thief comes only in order to steal and kill and destroy. I came that they may have and enjoy life, and have it in abundance (to the full, till it overflows)" (John 10:10).

2. "But You, O Lord, are a shield for me, my glory, and the lifter of my head" (Psalm 3:3).

3. "Nehemiah said, 'Go and enjoy choice food and sweet drinks, and send some to those who have nothing prepared. This day is sacred to our Lord. Do not grieve, for the joy of the LORD is your strength'" (Nehemiah 8:10 NIV).

4. *Matthew Henry's Concise Commentary on the Whole Bible*, http://bible.crosswalk.com/Commentaries/MatthewHenryConcise/mhc-con.cgi?book=1th&chapter=005, s.v. "1 Thessalonians 5:16–22."

5. "Every man to whom God has given riches and possessions, and the power to enjoy them and to accept his appointed lot and to rejoice in his toil—this is the gift of God [to him]" (Ecclesiastes 5:19).

About the Author

⌒

Joyce Meyer has been teaching the Word of God since 1976 and in full-time ministry since 1980. She is the best-selling author of more than fifty inspirational books, including *How to Hear from God, Knowing God Intimately,* and *Battlefield of the Mind.* She has also released thousands of teaching cassettes and a complete video library. Joyce's *Enjoying Everyday Life* radio and television programs are broadcast around the world, and she travels extensively conducting Joyce Meyer Ministries conferences. Joyce and her husband, Dave, are the parents of four grown children and make their home in St. Louis, Missouri.

To contact the author write:

Joyce Meyer Ministries
P. O. Box 655
Fenton, Missouri 63026

or call: (636) 349-0303

Internet Address: www.joycemeyer.org

Please include your testimony of help received from this book when you write. Your prayer requests are welcome.

To contact the ministry in Canada, please write:

Joyce Meyer Ministries, Inc.
Lambeth Box 1300
London, ON N6P 1T5
Canada

or call: (636) 349-0303

In Australia, please write:

Joyce Meyer Ministries, Inc.
Locked Bag 77
Mansfield Delivery Centre
Queensland 4122
Australia

or call: 07 3349 1200

In England, please write:

Joyce Meyer Ministries, Inc.
P. O. Box 1549
Windsor
SL4 1GT
United Kingdom

or call: (0) 1753-831102

Other Books by Joyce Meyer

〜

How to Hear from God

Knowing God Intimately

The Power of Forgiveness

The Power of Determination

The Power of Being Positive

The Secrets of Spiritual Power

The Battle Belongs to the Lord

Secrets to Exceptional Living

Eight Ways to Keep the Devil Under Your Feet

Teenagers Are People Too!

Filled with the Spirit

Celebration of Simplicity

The Joy of Believing Prayer

Never Lose Heart

Being the Person God Made You to Be

A Leader in the Making

"Good Morning, This Is God!" Gift Book

Jesus—Name Above All Names

"Good Morning, This Is God!" Daily Calendar

Help Me—I'm Married!

Reduce Me to Love
Be Healed in Jesus' Name
How to Succeed at Being Yourself
Eat and Stay Thin
Weary Warriors, Fainting Saints
Life in the Word Journal
Life in the Word Devotional
Be Anxious for Nothing
Be Anxious for Nothing Study Guide
Straight Talk on Loneliness
Straight Talk on Fear
Straight Talk on Insecurity
Straight Talk on Discouragement
Straight Talk on Worry
Straight Talk on Depression
Straight Talk on Stress
Don't Dread
Managing Your Emotions
Healing the Brokenhearted
"Me and My Big Mouth!"
"Me and My Big Mouth!" Study Guide
Prepare to Prosper
Do It Afraid!
Expect a Move of God in Your Life . . . Suddenly!
Enjoying Where You Are on the Way to Where You Are Going
The Most Important Decision You Will Ever Make
When, God, When?
Why, God, Why?
The Word, The Name, The Blood

Battlefield of the Mind

Battlefield of the Mind Study Guide

Tell Them I Love Them

Peace

The Root of Rejection

Beauty for Ashes

If not for the Grace of God

If not for the Grace of God Study Guide

Don't miss this upcoming book!

IN PURSUIT *of* PEACE
Joyce Meyer

Peace is a priority for God. Therefore it should be a priority for us as well. Indeed, we are instructed to seek peace with others. But in today's world, tranquility is hard to come by. If we don't have it ourselves, seeking it with others is an impossible task.

How do we find the calm and quiet we need in our lives? In her latest book, Joyce Meyer discusses the pursuit of true peace. Journey with her and learn how to:

- *Be at peace with yourself*—and how to make time for yourself and God
- *Develop a peaceful attitude*—and understand God's importance in your pursuit of peace
- *Enjoy peaceful relationships*—and how to maintain them
- *Be led by peace*—and discover how a peace-filled attitude affects every aspect of your life
- *And much more!*

IN PURSUIT OF PEACE shows us step by step how to live a life of peace, as God intended. The choice is ours to make, Joyce says. Are you ready?

COMING OCTOBER 2004